THEOLOGICAL

DILEMMAS

Gregory C. Higgins

PAULIST PRESS
New York/Mahwah

All scripture quotations, unless otherwise indicated, are taken from *The New American Bible*.

Library of Congress Cataloging-in-Publication Data

Higgins, Gregory C., 1960–
    Twelve theological dilemmas/Gregory C. Higgins.
        p.   cm.
    Includes bibliographical references.
    ISBN 0-8091-3232-X
    1. Theology, Doctrinal—Popular works.   2. Catholic Church—Doctrines—Popular works.   I. Title.   II. Title: 12 theological dilemmas.
BX1754.H52   1991
230′.2—dc20
                                                            91–4514
                                                             CIP

Published by Paulist Press
997 Macarthur Boulevard
Mahwah, New Jersey 07430

Printed and bound in the United States of America

Contents

Preface

This text has emerged out of my experience of teaching theology to high school students. In working through various theological questions with my students, I have found that I continually preface our discussions with a general observation about theology: namely, that often in theological discussions there is more than one consistent, reasonable position. Students examining such exchanges must therefore weigh the relative strengths and weaknesses of each position before choosing one from among the various possibilities. The final determination of what one takes to be the right theological position will depend a great deal upon what that person values theologically. This text provides an opportunity for readers to work through twelve theological dilemmas so that they can identify and scrutinize their own theological preferences.

This text will, I hope, be useful in three different settings: the school, the church, and the home. Those who teach introductory courses in theology to senior high school students or college freshmen must, within a relatively short period of time, present a comprehensive overview of Christian theology and prepare students for further theological study. Use of the following dilemma approach will, I believe, assist the educator to accomplish both tasks. The dilemmas can be utilized by the instructor to provide a general framework into which the current lectures and readings can be integrated while also serving as a means of helping students later recall the issues discussed in the course. Second, adult education coordinators in the local parishes face a different set of challenges. Adult education must be interesting and informative without being overly time-consuming. The program should also interest a wide range of people, yet be focused and directed. Depending on the length of the program, the group could center discussion on a certain number of chapters during each session. Third, this text may prove helpful to those who enjoy pondering and discussing theological questions, but do not have the time to attend classes or read works by several authors. The chapters concisely present the rival positions in each dilemma. Suggestions for further reading follow at the end of each chapter so that readers may pursue those topics which they find most interesting.

A few comments about style and format are in order. I have minimized the use of technical language. Of the many theological dilemmas which could be discussed, I have selected twelve. I have chosen these twelve from various disciplines within theology (biblical studies, ethics, systematic theology, etc.). As one would expect, issues discussed in one chapter will overlap with issues discussed in other chapters. It will be obvious at times that the context out of which these questions have emerged is a Roman Catholic one, though I feel that all of the chapters could be used in a Protestant or ecumenical gathering. In whatever setting it is read, I hope this text will bring the reader a deeper understanding and appreciation of theological reflection.

In closing, I would like to thank a number of people. First of all, I need to thank my students, both past and present, without whom this book would never have been written. I would also like to thank my colleagues at Christian Brothers Academy in Lincroft, NJ and my fellow parishioners at St. Rose of Lima in Freehold, NJ for their support over the years. I owe a debt of gratitude to Eileen Conway, Michael Ewing, Leslie Griffin, Joe Incandela, and Fr. James Massa for reading all or part of the manuscript and offering their very helpful comments and suggestions. Special thanks to Mary Trank for her assistance. Finally, I would like to thank my family, most especially my mother and father to whom I lovingly dedicate this work.

Introduction
What Is a Theological Dilemma?

A dilemma requires that a person make a choice between a number of desirable options. The one making this decision must weigh the advantages and disadvantages of each side and choose the better course of action while recognizing that each option has its drawbacks. For example, a young working couple with a newborn faces the difficult question of child-care. Should the mother or father stay at home with the child? If one of the parents stays at home with the newborn, can they do without the second income? If both parents work, does the child suffer in any way? This decision involves weighing a number of factors, e.g. the welfare of the child, income, the availability and cost of day care, and alternative day care possibilities. For some couples, this is not a dilemma. They clearly prefer one choice and consider the drawbacks inconsequential. Other couples agonize over this decision. For them, this is a dilemma of the highest order.

A person reflecting on questions about the Bible, Jesus, or the church must likewise choose one position from among the many available options. This critical reflection on one's religious beliefs and practices is called theology. The term "critical" is not meant pejoratively; it simply means that judgments are made about the subject matter. At times the right choice may seem obvious. There are, however, instances when the choice of one position entails the rejection of a desirable alternative. This is a theological dilemma. This text focuses on twelve such dilemmas.

The examination of these dilemmas affords the reader the

opportunity to reflect on several areas of Christian belief. Such reflection is the responsibility of all Christians. Too often Christians feel that theological reflection must be reserved solely for professional theologians. Theological literature often contributes to this unfortunate situation. The titles seem foreboding, the subject matter esoteric, and the language incomprehensible. As a result, many believers feel removed from the ongoing theological discussion within their own religious communities. They shy away from theological reflection, preferring instead to leave such questioning to those with advanced degrees.

In that situation, three parties suffer: the individual, the church, and the theologians. First of all, individual Christians are deprived of the opportunity to acquire a deeper understanding of Christianity. When Christians examine their beliefs, new insights can emerge. Over time these insights build on one another. This process enables the believer to come to a renewed understanding of the faith. Second, the Christian church suffers when theological reflection becomes the exclusive domain of some "elite." The health of the church depends on the presence of a well-informed, curious body of believers. Theological discussion contributes to the formation of that group. The exclusion of the non-professional from both the struggle and the reward of theological reflection creates a gap between scholarship and church life. Finally, the theologians themselves suffer the loss of the input of those living the very faith that is the object of their inquiry. Shifts in theology often arise out of the experience of the Christian communities as they struggle to implement the gospel message in their own lives. In our own day and age, the movement known as liberation theology dramatically testifies to this interaction between theology and the lived experience of Christians. Liberation theology grew out of the experience of the poor in Latin American as they struggled to relate the gospel to their struggle for economic and political justice in their countries.

The following chapters serve as an invitation to participate in theological reflection through an examination of twelve theological dilemmas. As in the case of the young couple making choices concerning child-care, there might be times when the choice will be easily made. At other times, the dilemma might not be so easily resolved. Whatever the case may be, it is my hope that these chapters will serve as the basis for profitable theological reflection and discussion.

The Dilemma of Christology

What did Jesus know, and when?

Who was Jesus of Nazareth? The force of this question has not been diminished by time. It remains as intriguing and relevant a question for Christians today as it was for those who walked with him on the dusty roads of Palestine two thousand years ago. The traditional affirmation about Jesus Christ is that he was fully human and fully divine. It is this central Christian doctrine which serves as the starting point for our examination of theological dilemmas.

Christology, which literally means "the study of Christ," is the technical expression for an examination of the person of Jesus. There are, generally speaking, two approaches in christology. These approaches correspond to the affirmation that Jesus was both fully human and fully divine. A "low christology" or "christology from below" emphasizes the humanity of Jesus. A "high christology" or "christology from above" emphasizes the divinity of Jesus. A low christology does not deny the divinity of Jesus nor does a high christology deny the humanity of Jesus. Each approach affirms that Jesus was both fully human and fully divine, though each clearly attaches greater significance to one or the other.

In order to clarify the difference between a high and low christology, consider the following hypothetical question about Jesus' knowledge. Suppose everyone in the ancient world assumed that the world was flat. Did Jesus know that the world is round? Those who emphasize that Jesus was fully divine would likely conclude that Jesus possessed the same knowledge as

God. Since God is all-knowing and since God created the world, Jesus would know that the world is round. Those who emphasize that Jesus was fully human would likely conclude that Jesus shared in our limitations. Since the flatness of the world was an unquestioned assumption of those living in the first century, Jesus did not know that the world is round. Questions about Jesus' consciousness are purely matters of speculation. We have no evidence either way to decide the question. But this type of speculation does serve the very useful purpose of helping Christians determine whether they hold a high or low christology.

It would seem that questions of christology could be settled quite easily by scripture. Any appeal to scripture to solve our christological questions must, however, deal with two problems. First of all, the problem of the historical reliability of scripture needs to be addressed. Did Jesus actually speak the words recorded in scripture or were his words constructed by later gospel writers? For example, did Jesus know that he would be raised up on the third day? There clearly exists biblical testimony to the effect that Jesus did know of his resurrection well in advance of his crucifixion. In Mark's gospel, for instance, after Peter professes Jesus as messiah, Jesus "began to teach them that the Son of Man had to suffer much, be rejected by the elders, the chief priests, and the scribes, be put to death, and rise three days later" (Mk 8:31). This clearly suggests that Jesus was fully aware of the events which would take place before and after his death. It might be the case, however, that such verses reflect the post-resurrection knowledge of the early Christians rather than the foreknowledge of the historical Jesus looking ahead to the cross. If the former is the case, citing a particular verse will not settle a christological debate.

The second problem one encounters with an appeal to scripture is the diversity of christologies within the scriptures themselves. One can appeal to any number of verses in support of either a low or a high christology. In support of a low christology, one could point to the story of Jesus overturning the tables of the money-changers in the temple. In this scene Jesus was given to the same emotions, feelings of indignation, and spontaneous outbursts as any of us. Equally familiar, however, is the story of Jesus walking on the water. This story presents a Jesus with abilities uniquely divine. His other miracles, as well, set him apart from the rest of humanity. Given the presence of both christologies in the scriptures, again it is the case that an appeal to any single verse will not in itself settle a christological debate.

With the acknowledgement of those two problems, an examination of the relative strengths and weaknesses of a low and a high christology can now begin. Proponents of a low christology need to respond to the valid criticisms of the proponents of a high christology (and vice versa). In this way, both parties might gain new insight into Jesus of Nazareth.

A low christology presents Jesus as one who fully experienced the heights and depths of human existence. As a boy he played in the fields with his friends; as a grown man he celebrated at weddings. The image of Jesus surrounded by children conveys a sense of warmth and playfulness. Jesus' life was not one untouched by pain. He grieved at the death of his friend Lazarus. He was betrayed by a disciple. In the garden of Gethsemani he agonized over his impending death and while undergoing the painfully slow death of crucifixion cried out, "My God, my God, why have you forsaken me?"

Many Christians feel a kinship with this human Jesus who experienced the joys and pains of human existence. He shared fully their human condition and out of that preached a message of love for all humanity. To illustrate his points he drew upon occurrences in the daily lives of the people around him: a shepherd who lost a sheep, a woman who lost a coin, a traveler attacked by robbers. His temptations were not simply casual or momentary distractions; they were alluring options for his life which he renounced. For those struggling with important life questions, the idea that Jesus underwent this type of struggle is an appealing notion. They feel a bond with this human Jesus.

The popular image of the human Jesus which emerges from the gospels is of a man filled with compassion. For instance, in Mark's gospel a leper approaches Jesus and humbly professes, "If you will to do so, you can cure me" (1:41). The gospel writer continues, "Moved with pity, Jesus stretched out his hand, touched him, and said, 'I do will it.' " In this passage Jesus is deeply moved by the physical suffering of others. Elsewhere he is compassionate to those who have failed morally. Jesus saves the life of the woman caught in the act of adultery by challenging her accusers, "Let the man among you who has no sin be the first to cast a stone at her" (Jn 8:7). The scene concludes with Jesus asking, "Has no one condemned you?" "No one, sir," she answered. Jesus said, "Nor do I condemn you. You may go. But from now on, avoid this sin" (Jn 8:10–11).

Critics charge that a low christology has a number of drawbacks. First of all, an emphasis on Jesus' humanity runs the danger of compromising the uniqueness of Jesus. Jesus becomes simply a great teacher, a person of lasting historical significance, or a wise sage. Jesus becomes no different than Socrates: a wise person of great insight who courageously accepted death rather than compromise his principles. Does a low christology give an adequate account of salvation? Can Jesus, the teacher par excellence, be the savior of the world? Can Jesus, the Galilean prophet, forgive us of our sins or reconcile the world to the Father? This activity seems to rely upon an understanding of Jesus as God's Son. Does a low christology compromise a necessary element of Christianity: that "it is in Christ and through his blood that we have been redeemed and our sins forgiven" (Eph 1:7)?

The second criticism concerns the reliability of Jesus'

teaching. A low christology underscores Jesus' humanity, and an essential dimension of being human is limitation. Humans do not possess complete knowledge. Humans can be in error. In a low christology, is it possible that Jesus was in error? Aristotle was a genius, but shared in the limited knowledge of his day. Newton was surpassed by Einstein. Was Jesus correct in all his teachings? If he was wrong at times, which teachings were right? How does one distinguish right from wrong teachings?

The final question concerns Jesus' holiness. If we assign Jesus the emotion of compassion or pity, can we be justified in excluding the emotions of greed and jealousy? The implication of a low christology is that we must admit all emotions which humans experience as possible experiences of Jesus. Does that in any way diminish the holiness of Jesus? This raises the question of Jesus' sinlessness. The letter to the Hebrews states that Jesus was "one who was tempted in every way that we are, yet never sinned" (4:15). Did Jesus sin? Was Jesus unable to sin? Was Jesus able to sin, yet freely chose not to sin?

Advocates of a high christology feel that their perspective avoids many of the criticisms leveled against a low christology. They emphasize that Jesus was not merely an enlightened mortal. He was truly God's Son who fully revealed the will of the Father to us. Jesus is, as the Nicene Creed makes clear, "God from God, Light from Light, true God from true God." When Jesus Christ walked this earth, those who encountered him met not only a man of great wisdom, they met God's only Son. The gospel with the highest christology is undoubtedly John's gospel. Echoing the words of the creation story in Genesis, John begins, "In the beginning was the Word and the Word was in God's presence, and the Word was God" (1:1). In John's gospel, Jesus is this Word of God who was present to God at creation and came into the world to reveal the will of the Father to us. "The Word became flesh and made his dwelling among us . . ." (1:14a). This event of God's Word becoming flesh is known as the incarnation. As the Incarnate Word, Jesus announces, "The Father and I are one" (Jn 10:30).

In a high christology, Jesus is distinct in kind from any other person who walked the face of the earth. He is not only a wise sage or a charismatic preacher; he is God's only Son. "He is the image of the invisible God, the first-born of all creatures. In him everything in heaven and on earth was created, things visible and invisible, whether thrones or dominations, principalities or powers; all were created through him, and for him. He is before all else that is. In him everything continues in being" (Col 1:15–17). His coming was foretold by the prophets, and while on earth he worked miracles and called upon people to have faith in him. Christians proclaim him as the light of the world, the true vine, and the good shepherd. Jesus sits at the right hand of the Father, and at the end of time Jesus will stand as judge over all the world.

Those favoring a high christology contend that a number of appealing consequences follow from this understanding of Jesus. First of all, a high christology makes it clear that Jesus' message is nothing less than the word of God. We are assured of the truth of Jesus' teaching for the simple reason that the words are those of God's only Son. Jesus, as the second person of the Trinity, reveals the will of the Father to us. This message is not bound by the constraints of the time in which it was first delivered. The message of Jesus is eternally true and binding on all Christians during any time period. The teachings of Jesus will not be overturned or amended at some later date. Second, the incarnation also reveals the love God has for the world. God took on flesh and dwelt among us. God did not reject the world, but became a part of it and in doing so affirmed the beauty and goodness of the created order. Third, we have the promise of eternal life from the lips of the savior himself. "In my Father's house there are many dwelling places; otherwise, how could I have told you that I was going to prepare a place for you? I am indeed going to prepare a place for you, and then I shall come back to take you with me, that where I am you also may be" (Jn 14:3–4). We have the assurance that sin and death will be overcome.

Critics charge that a high christology runs into two difficulties. The first concerns Jesus himself and the other involves our relationship to Jesus. The first point of concern is whether Jesus' divinity overpowered his humanity. The church in its teachings insists that this did not occur. At the Council of Chalcedon in 451 the bishops stated that Jesus possessed full humanity and full divinity "without confusion." We can only speculate, as we did earlier, whether there would not be times when the two would seem diametrically opposed. The second concern involves Jesus' otherworldliness. A high christology runs the risk of removing Jesus from the human condition and setting his life apart from our own. We can certainly give praise and honor to the Word Incarnate, but can we relate our life and its concerns to those of Jesus? If we are admonished to love our enemies as Jesus did, we might retort, "Well, it was easy for him. He was God."

This, then, is the dilemma: Is Jesus best thought of in terms of a high christology or a low christology? An initial response might be to find a middle way between the two, preserving the advantages of each. A developmental christology is sometimes proposed as a middle way between the low and high christologies. Referring back to the question of Jesus' knowledge of the future, a developmental christology suggests that Jesus grew in awareness of his own identity. Jesus came to the realization of his identity gradually over the course of time. At some point Jesus gained a complete understanding of his identity. This view preserves both the human struggle (low christology) with the awareness of divinity (high christology). This developmental christology, however, does not resolve all the possible questions. At which point in time did Jesus realize his true identity? Was it when Jesus was a boy or when he began his ministry? Once Jesus realized his divinity was he any less human? Can a divine being be fearful of death in the same way that humans are? Any "middle way" christology would always be subject to the question, "But wasn't Jesus human?" or "But wasn't Jesus divine?" These christologies answer certain questions, but not all. There seems to be an inevitable tension between Jesus' humanity and divinity, and all christologies tend to give more weight to one over the other.

One final observation must be made. After examining the advantages and disadvantages of the different christologies the question often arises whether we in fact create a Jesus to our own liking. In the name of the Jesus they find in the scriptures, Christians have launched crusades and burned heretics, founded hospitals and educated the poor. Do Christians who favor a low christology ignore the verses supporting a high christology (and vice versa)? If so, is this selective reading of scripture creating a one-sided picture of Jesus? This clearly is a danger. The diversity of christological statements in scripture (not to mention in Christian literature), however, does not have to be seen as a liability. First of all, the mystery of the person of Jesus Christ is inexhaustible. To expect one image or one perspective to capture fully the depth and richness of the prophet from Nazareth is unrealistic. Second, there is truth found in both low and high christologies. The tension between the two is a healthy one. It promotes ongoing reflection and refinement of earlier positions.

Christological questions present us with a dilemma. On the one hand, we relate with the human Jesus who underwent struggles and emerged as a man of principle and a preacher of love and justice. On the other hand, we revere the majestic Son of God who came down to earth to reveal God's love for the world. Some type of trade-off is unavoidable in christology. If we prefer a high christology, we must deal with the possible loss of his humanity. If we prefer a low christology, we must deal with the possible loss of his divinity. Such is the nature of a theological dilemma.

DISCUSSION QUESTIONS

1. Do you prefer a high or low christology? Why?
2. What objections could be raised to your position? How would you respond?
3. Which gospel story do you find most appealing? Why?
4. When Jesus was a small boy, did he know that Judas would betray him?

SUGGESTED READING

Gerard Sloyan's *Jesus in Focus: A Life in its Setting* (Mystic: Twenty-Third Publications, 1983), written for a general audience, offers a number of portraits of Jesus.

What Are They Saying About Jesus? by Gerald O'Collins, S.J. (New York: Paulist, 1977) is a fine, short introduction to the "state of the question."

Who Is This Christ? by Reginald Fuller and Pheme Perkins, two respected scholars in the field (Philadelphia: Fortress, 1983), reviews the biblical writings.

Jesus Before Christianity (Maryknoll: Orbis, 1976) by Albert Nolan concentrates on the social and political dimension of Jesus' ministry.

Jesus Through the Centuries by Jaroslav Pelikan (New Haven: Yale University Press, 1985) presents various christologies which have emerged throughout Christian history. It is the most difficult of the suggested books, but it makes for very rewarding reading.

The Dilemma of the Bible

Was the world really created in seven days?

The Bible is the word of God expressed in the words of humans. In this seemingly innocent theological claim is to be found the beginning of an intense theological controversy. Put simply, do we emphasize that the Bible is *the word of God* or that it is expressed in *the words of humans*? This difference may seem slight at first, but it becomes clear that each emphasis leads us to different conclusions about how the Bible should be read. It is helpful to approach this question by examining two popular, though different, ways of reading the Bible: the fundamentalist approach and the historical-critical approach.

Fundamentalists accent the first half of our opening statement: the Bible is *the word of God* in the words of humans. For the fundamentalist there is a direct connection between what God wants us to know and what is recorded in scripture. God, in effect, speaks directly to us through the pages of the Bible. Since God does not err, the Bible is free from error. Since God does not deceive, the Bible means what it says. Two practical consequences follow from these beliefs. The first is that the Bible can never be wrong about anything. Often fundamentalists will refer to the "inerrancy" of scripture, by which they mean that all information contained in the Bible (e.g. historical, ethical, scientific) is without error. Second, since the Bible means what it says, all the biblical stories are literally true (e.g. Noah's ark, the tower of Babel). All the events recorded in the Bible actually occurred in the manner described in the scriptures; therefore, the Bible should be read literally.

15

Although they acknowledge that the Bible was indeed composed by humans, the fundamentalists maintain that the biblical authors were inspired by the Holy Spirit to write the words they did. Consequently the work they produced is said to be inspired writing. As is written in 2 Timothy, "All scripture is inspired of God and is useful for teaching—for reproof, correction, and training in holiness so that the man of God may be fully competent and equipped for every good work" (3:16). This verse supports two important fundamentalist tenets: the first is that the Bible is divinely inspired, the second is that the Bible offers sound teachings for all generations. The central fundamentalist beliefs follow from this theory of divine inspiration: As a divinely inspired text, the Bible is free from all error; since the Bible is free from error, it should be read literally. Furthermore, the biblical authors did not put in written form their own private ideas and wishes, but rather God's will. Since God's will does not change, the Bible is a source of timeless ethical truths.

Advocates of the historical-critical approach emphasize that the Bible is the word of God expressed *in the words of humans*. For them, the biblical writings have emerged out of a very long process of human composition. Most importantly, they claim that in order to understand the biblical writings the reader must first situate them in the historical setting of the time in which they were written. This historical-critical approach attempts to learn as much as possible about the culture in which various texts were written. What were the political, social, and economic conditions? What writing style was common to them? How did they pass on stories? The historical-critical reader approaches the biblical writings with the knowledge gained by asking these types of questions. This approach also makes a distinction between "what actually happened" and "what is recorded in scripture." In many cases those two things will be identical, but it is also possible that the scriptural story has embellished the actual historical account or perhaps the scriptural story is speaking symbolically rather than historically.

The story of the crossing of the Red (or Reed) Sea provides a helpful illustration of how the fundamentalist and the historical-critical reader approach the biblical stories differently. In this story Moses and his people flee from slavery in Egypt and the Egyptians pursue them. The Lord then commands Moses to raise his staff to part the waters of the Red Sea. After the Hebrews have passed through on the dry ground between the walls of water, Moses lowers his hands and the water flows back to its normal height, drowning the Egyptians. The fundamentalist regards the story as an accurate historical account of the exodus from Egypt. The historical-critical reader, by contrast, may claim that the event was actually a quick change in the tides which the Hebrews attributed to the might of the Lord.

The historical-critical reader charges that the fundamentalist approach inadequately deals with three problems. The first is the presence of contradictions or inconsistencies in the Bible. The second is the influence of culture on the biblical writings themselves. The third is the presence of literary devices in the Bible.

The historical-critical readers of the Bible argue that the first problem with fundamentalism is that it overlooks the obvious: the Bible does not always agree with itself. For example, fundamentalists often refer to Genesis when dealing with questions about creation and evolution. The problem is that Genesis contains not one creation story, but two. The first creation story runs from Genesis 1:1–2:4a. The second creation story runs from Genesis 2:4b–25. Without going into great detail, the two creation stories differ in many ways. For example, Adam is created in 2:7 after God has already created man and woman in 1:27. The first story, which is very structured, describes the transformation of the earth from a "formless wasteland" into a bountiful abode for man and woman who were created on the sixth day. The seventh day is a day of rest. The second story resembles a folktale. Here readers find the familiar story of the garden of Eden with the tree of life at its center and the tree of knowledge of good and evil of which Adam and Eve may not eat. God's actions are described in anthropomorphic terms: God forms the man out of clay, walks through the garden, and calls out to Adam who is hiding from God after eating from the forbidden tree.

According to the historical-critical readers, the presence of two creation stories argues against the fundamentalist claim that the Bible should be read literally. Clearly if those responsible for the final edition of Genesis intended to recount the origin of the universe or the appearance of humanity on the earth, they would not have begun Genesis with two conflicting creation stories. They would have harmonized the two stories or accepted one over the other. Those favoring the historical-critical approach argue that the presence of two creation stories would be more understandable if the editors' intention was to teach a religious lesson rather than provide a scientific account of the origin of the universe. For example, the first creation story parallels in many ways a popular creation story in Babylon where the Jews were taken into exile in 587 B.C. and as such serves two important functions. First, it offers hope to those in exile. Just as Yahweh brought the universe out of the primordial chaos, so too will God bring order out of the chaos of the exile. Second, the story serves an educational purpose in that it demonstrates the differences between the beliefs of the Babylonians and those of the Jews. The most important of these is monotheism. Yahweh alone rules the universe; there is no equal force which battles God for control.

Readers of the Bible discover another scriptural inconsistency in the four gospels' record of Jesus' last words. In Matthew and Mark, Jesus cries out, "My God, my God, why have you forsaken me?" (Mk 15:34; Mt 27:46). In Luke, he says,

"Father, into your hands I commend my spirit" (Lk 23:46). Finally in John, Jesus stoically states, "It is finished" (Jn 19:30). Historical-critical readers of the Bible suggest that if the fundamentalists were correct about scripture there would be a much higher degree of similarity between the various accounts of an event of such lasting importance as Jesus' last words before his death.

The second problem with the fundamentalist perspective according to the historical-critical reader concerns the influence of culture on the biblical writings. Put simply, the fundamentalist contends that the biblical writings reflect the will of God for all ages. The historical-critical reader argues that the biblical writings reflect the values and beliefs of the culture in which they were produced. This difference results in conflicting understandings of a number of the ethical teachings found in the Bible. As discussed earlier, the fundamentalist insists that the Bible be read literally. The fundamentalist regards the Bible as the ethical standard by which all beliefs and practices are to be measured. This standard does not change. What is wrong in God's eyes in one age does not become right in the next. People may, as a result of sin, mistakenly believe that a given action is morally correct, but if it violates a scriptural command, it is immoral.

The historical-critical reader, by contrast, believes that certain biblical passages reflect a cultural attitude or custom of the time rather than God's will. This can be illustrated by citing passages concerning women, slaves, and warfare. In 1 Corinthians, Paul sets down the following rule: "According to the rule observed in all the assemblies of believers, women should keep silent in such gatherings. They may not speak. Rather, as the law states, submissiveness is indicated for them. If they want to learn anything, they should ask their husbands at home. It is a disgrace when a woman speaks in the assembly" (14:33–35). The author of 1 Timothy offers similar advice to the worshiping community: "A woman must learn in silence and be submissive. I do not permit a woman to act as teacher, or in any way to have authority over a man; she must be quiet. For Adam was created first, Eve afterward; moreover, it was not Adam who was deceived but the woman" (2:11–14). In the letter to the Ephesians, slaves are encouraged to submit to their masters: "Slaves, obey your human masters with the reverence, the awe, and the sincerity you owe to Christ" (6:5). Finally, in the story of the taking of Jericho the city is placed "under the Lord's ban." This meant that all humans and livestock in the city were to be killed. This slaughter was carried out in the name of God. "They observed the ban by putting to the sword all living creatures in the city: men and women, young and old, as well as oxen, sheep, and asses" (Jos 6:21).

The historical-critical approach situates those practices and attitudes in the social context of the time in which they were written. They do not regard such passages as timeless divine truths, but rather as expressions of antiquated cultural beliefs and practices. According to the fundamentalist, when the Bible conflicts with our beliefs, we must always defer to the literal statements of the Bible. For the fundamentalist, the story of Adam and Eve, not the work of Charles Darwin, accurately describes how humans came to walk on this earth. For this reason they oppose the use of textbooks which teach the theory of evolution. The teaching of evolution in public school classrooms represents a move away from biblical truth and consequently should be fought at every turn. The historical-critical readers argue, however, that if the Bible is the word of God *in the words of humans*, then the biblical writings will inevitably reflect the authors' understanding of the world. The creation stories, when situated in their original historical context, provide us with rich insights into the centrality of monotheism, the pervasiveness of evil, and the need to be stewards of God's creation. What is not required, however, is a rejection of the theory of the "Big Bang" or a disregard of fossil data simply because that information clashes with a literal reading of the scriptures. Christians may both accept the theory of evolution and maintain the truthfulness of the Bible's teachings. Second, Christians may also acknowledge the impact of culture on the biblical writings, yet not feel called upon to support an attitude or practice which they find objectionable. For example, Christians need not accept the patriarchical attitudes about the place of women in society which found their way into the biblical writings. In this way, the importance of the Bible is preserved and the insights gained since the time of the biblical writings are also treasured.

The third historical-critical objection to fundamentalism is a literary one. In our everyday speech, for example, we recognize that not all expressions are meant to be taken literally (e.g. "It's raining cats and dogs"). In the same way, the biblical expression "forty days" may not mean a literal forty days, but rather may express, in the popular language of the ancient world, a long period of time. By allowing for a non-literal reading of a biblical expression, the historical-critical reader expands the range of possible interpretations of any biblical passage. An example of this is the troubling admonition, "If your right eye is your trouble, gouge it out and throw it away. Better to lose part of your body than to have it all cast into Gehenna" (Mt 5:29). By allowing for the use of hyperbole, the historical-critical reader might regard such a passage as a call to live a life of purity and righteousness, while in no way expecting a person to follow the command literally. The story of Jesus' temptations in the desert provides another example of literary license. It is possible that Jesus may not have actually gone into the desert for forty days and engaged the devil in conversation. Even if the story is historically false, it faithfully captures a sense of the struggle Jesus underwent before his public ministry.

The fundamentalists are not without responses to the questions raised by their critics. First, they disregard the historical-critical distinction between "what really happened" and "what the Bible says." As the inspired word of God, the Bible means what it says and says what it means. The fundamentalists argue that their concepts of inspiration and inerrancy present a coherent, sensible account of how God speaks to the world. Fundamentalists believe that the historical-critical approach does not offer an intelligible theory of inspiration. In what sense can we Christians speak of the scriptures as divinely inspired if not in a straightforward, literal sense?

The fundamentalists also counter their opponents by asking them to identify the standards by which they differentiate those biblical passages which reflect the will of God from those which reflect the thinking of the time in which they were written. Two areas of particular interest are miracles and ethics. In terms of miracles, the fundamentalists ask, "Should we reject the historical accuracy of those biblical stories which we believe to be scientifically impossible (e.g. Jesus walking on water)?" If we judge the truth or falsity of the biblical stories by this scientific criterion, charge the fundamentalists, we must disregard all of the miracle stories in the Bible. What becomes of Christ's virgin birth or his resurrection? The fundamentalists also warn that readers of the Bible might choose to accept the ethical teachings which agree with their own morality and ignore the ethical teachings which they find troublesome. The fundamentalists argue that a consistent application of the theory of inspiration to all the biblical writings avoids this most perplexing problem of deciding which passages are divinely inspired and which are culturally conditioned.

Despite the differences between the fundamentalist approach and the historical-critical approach, there is one important area of agreement between the two. Advocates of both approaches accord the Bible a unique, privileged status. Like all great literary works, the Bible provides the readers with a glimpse into the human condition. Like other important works, the Bible has far-reaching cultural influence. For Christians, however, the Bible is not simply another classic of western culture or lesson in ancient history. The Bible tells the story of God's relationship with humanity which reaches its culmination in the person of Jesus. Fundamentalists and historical-critical readers seem to agree on little else, but this point of agreement provides some basis for discussion between the two parties.

When reading the Bible we confront a dilemma. If we accept the literal truth of all the biblical stories, then we must deal with the ensuing variance between the modern mindset and many biblical presuppositions, stories, and attitudes. On the other hand, if we allow that certain stories reflect the worldview of the cultures in which they were written, we then face the difficult task of distinguishing the cultural elements from the divine elements in the biblical text. This dilemma positions us between regarding the Bible as a sacred text which demands our allegiance and a human text which invites our scrutiny.

DISCUSSION QUESTIONS

1. Which approach to reading the scriptures do you prefer? Why?
2. How do you respond to the objections from the other side?
3. Did Jesus walk on water?
4. Are there any biblical stories which you feel are not based in historical fact?

SUGGESTED READING

For a short statement of the fundamentalist position, see the excerpt from the Emmaus Bible School in *Constructing a Life Philosophy,* ed. David L. Bender (St. Paul: Greenhaven Press, 1985) 90–96.

Rudolf Bultmann's essay "New Testament and Mythology" in *Kerygma and Myth,* ed. Hans Werner Bartsch (New York: Harper & Row, 1961), is the classic statement of the problem.

Richard Chilson's *Full Christianity: A Catholic Response to Fundamental Questions* (Mahwah: Paulist Press, 1985) and Philip St. Romain's *Catholic Answers to Fundamentalists' Questions* (Liguori: Liguori Publications, 1984) both address the challenge of fundamentalism in a very readable fashion.

For advanced theological students, "Cosmology, Ontology, and the Travail of Biblical Language" by Langdon Gilkey *Journal of Religion* 41(3), 1961, offers an excellent summary of the problems discussed in this chapter.

The Dilemma of God's Presence

How does God speak to us?

What relationship does God have with humanity? How do people come to an experience of God? This chapter examines two prominent responses within the Christian tradition to these two interrelated questions. One response emphasizes the distinction between God and humanity. Unlike humans, God possesses unlimited knowledge, power, and love. This response highlights the transcendence of God. In this understanding of the divine-human relationship, the proper human response to God is obedience. The second response emphasizes the union of God and humanity. God's presence fills the world, and humans experience that presence in a number of ways. This response highlights the immanence of God. In this understanding of the divine-human relationship, the proper human response to God is cooperation. In this chapter we analyze these two understandings of God's relationship to humanity. We begin by examining two scriptural stories: the first highlights God's transcendence, the second God's immanence.

God's transcendence is stressed in the closing chapters of the book of Job. Here the innocent Job is no longer content to suffer in silence and endure the endless chatter of his misguided friends. Job demands a hearing before God. A storm develops and God's voice bellows from the clouds, "Where were you when I founded the earth? Tell me if you have understanding" (38:4). God proceeds to enumerate the divine feats which no human could accomplish or fully comprehend. All human achievement pales in comparison with the creation of

25

the world and all its inhabitants. God is the creator and we are the created. Job can only humbly acknowledge God's point: "Behold, I am of little account; what can I answer you? I put my hand over my mouth" (40:4). The Judaeo-Christian tradition has consistently affirmed the truth of the closing chapters of the book of Job which speak of God's awesome power and wisdom. We are not God; we are God's servants.

The Judaeo-Christian tradition has equally maintained the truth that "the Lord is near to all who call upon him, to all who call upon him in truth" (Ps 145:18). In contrast to the book of Job, for example, a scene from the book of 1 Kings offers another image of God's presence. At one point, Elijah stands at the very mountain where Moses received the law. The Lord instructs Elijah, "Go outside and stand on the mountain before the Lord; the Lord will be passing by" (19:11). A strong and mighty wind arises, then an earthquake shakes the ground, and finally fire appears, but God is not found in any of them. Instead, "After the fire there was a tiny whispering sound. When he heard this, Elijah hid his face in his cloak and went and stood at the entrance of the cave" (19:12–13). It is in this tiny whispering sound that Elijah encounters God.

The biblical authors depict God's presence differently in the Job and Elijah stories. The author of Job highlights God's awesome, undefinable power and wisdom. God is beyond all of the categories which we can use to describe God. Those who think they have defined God are simply mistaken. No definition, description, or image will ever completely capture the unfathomable reality of God. This theme is also found in the book of Isaiah: " 'For my thoughts are not your thoughts, nor are your ways my ways,' says the Lord. 'As high as the heavens are above the earth, so high are my ways above your ways and my thoughts above your thoughts' " (Is 55:8–9). By contrast, the imagery of the Elijah story suggests an immanent view of God's presence in the world. The author first presents the typical images of transcendence. The imagery of wind, earthquakes, and fire recalls the giving of the law to Moses; in contrast to that event, Elijah encounters God in a gentle whisper. This image suggests that the presence of God is also encountered as a simple presence, a gentle power operating within the course of ordinary human experience. When we focus on the transcendence of God, we stand in awe and respect of God. God's immanence conveys a sense of intimacy and closeness which is lacking in the imagery of wind, earthquakes, and fire.

Whether God's presence is transcendent or immanent is not the dilemma. The Christian tradition has rightly affirmed that God's presence is both. The dilemma lies in deciding whether to emphasize one or the other. An emphasis on either pole results in a different view of the relationship between God and humanity. The emphasis on transcendence results in a relationship characterized by obedience while the emphasis on immanence results in a relationship characterized by cooperation. This connection between transcendence and obedience, on the one hand, and immanence and cooperation, on the other, requires further elaboration.

Those who emphasize the transcendence of God stress the otherness of God. God's utter majesty makes it abundantly clear that God is the ruler and we are the subjects. This theme is found in the story of Adam and Eve. In this mythical story the serpent lures Eve with the thought, "God knows that when you eat of it (i.e. the forbidden tree of knowledge) your eyes will be opened, and you will be like God, knowing good and evil" (Gn 3:5) RSV. In a garden filled with all good things, Adam and Eve desire God's knowledge. As a statement about human nature, the story argues that the fundamental flaw of humans is that we want to be God rather than God's servants. This theme reappears in the stories of idolatry in the Bible (e.g. the worship of the golden calf, Ex 32). We want to create a god to our liking and follow that god. We want God to fit into our scheme of things, rather than conform ourselves to God's will. The sin of idolatry is nothing less than the unwillingness to accept God on God's own terms. The worship of a golden calf or any other object is a futile attempt at controlling God or molding God to our desires. By emphasizing God's transcendence theologians seek to prevent such an abuse. God is the sovereign Lord of the universe and we are God's servants. The proper human response to God is therefore obedience.

An emphasis on the immanence of God presents a different model of the divine-human relationship. Here God's presence pervades the whole of human experience. God prods, lures, prompts, and invites humans to participate in the "deeper life," the creative, sustaining power underlying human existence. Humans, in their freedom, may elect to follow another course of action. Such a course of action would prove less beneficial to all parties concerned; perhaps the consequences would be disastrous. To choose a rather commonplace example, suppose a young man has a gift for writing. His poetry captures beautifully many of the emotions and feelings which seem to be adequately expressed only through poetry. After he graduates from college, he abandons his writing for more practical pursuits. Though drawn to the pen, he convinces himself that such writing must now cease so that he can devote his energies fully to other more financially rewarding activities. This small scale example of a person living a life of "quiet desperation" reminds us that we can ignore the deepest yearnings within ourselves. On a grander scale, we can do the same with the urgings of God. We can resist them or we can cooperate with them.

We now are able to tackle the question, "How do people come to an experience of God?" The metaphors of obedience and cooperation imply different answers to this question. If we are called to obey God, then there must be some way we can learn what God wishes us to do. There must be a source of some kind which links the transcendent God with humanity. An emphasis on God's immanence suggests that God can be discovered in a number of ways. God's presence is not revealed exclusively through one "privileged" source. Each of these points requires further clarification.

Those who emphasize God's transcendence insist that all knowledge of God is given to us by God. This model of the divine-human relationship requires a privileged source through which God's revelation can be delivered to humanity. There must be some point of contact between the transcendent God and this world. In Christian thought, the obvious connection is Jesus Christ, the eternal Word come down from heaven. "No one has ever seen God. It is God the only Son, ever at the Father's side, who has revealed him" (Jn 1:18). Others will argue that the Bible itself is the literal word of God and hence contains within it the will of God. Others will insist that certain ecclesiastical leaders or charismatic prophets are the means by which God speaks to humanity. In any event, there is a clearly defined bridge between the transcendent God and humanity.

When God's immanence is stressed, God's presence can be located within the wide range of human experience. It is not confined to any particular mode. God can be experienced in the traditional religious fashion: in private prayer, in liturgy, or through spiritual reading. God may also, however, be experienced in nature, in music, or in a great literary work. The wide range of human experience allows for contact with the divine presence subtly at work in the world. Picture the divine presence as a great underground spring. As one looks out upon a meadow with mountains in the background, one sees the various flowers which are in bloom in the meadow, the green grass which rolls toward the mountains, the mighty trees which have grown on the ridge, and the different strata of rock which have been eroded by the mountain stream. All of these natural beauties owe their existence to the underground stream. That one source has produced an array of beautiful objects. In the same way, God's presence manifests itself in assorted ways. There exists no special or privileged source. All literature, philosophy, art, and poetry can convey a sense of the divine in the midst of ordinary human experience.

Theologians on both sides of this dilemma acknowledge that their critics present reasonable challenges to their positions. Theologians favoring an accent on God's immanence acknowledge that a stress on transcendence serves as a wise safeguard against idolatry. We do indeed stand as God's servants—we heed, we do not create, God. Theologians who prefer to highlight the transcendence of God admit that the idea of seeing our lives as a cooperative effort with God presents an appealing portrait of the Christian life. Despite these concessions, both sides continue to present significant challenges to each other. We will examine two challenges from each side. We begin with two challenges to the transcendence camp. The first concerns the role of human responsibility, the second involves the means by which we come to knowledge of God.

The first challenge arises out of a concern to preserve a meaningful role for humans in the ongoing life of the world. If God is the sovereign Lord of the universe who alone possesses full knowledge, power, and love, then what place do humans have in the determination of the world's future? Has God predetermined events to follow a particular course? Can human choices alter the divine plan in any way? If God's power is seen as all-determining, then the events which take place *should* take place. This view of the divine-human relationship, charge critics, diminishes human responsibility for the present condition of the world and endorses a passive stance toward social injustice. Critics insist that the metaphor of cooperation promotes a better understanding of the necessary role humans play in the preservation and improvement of the world.

The second question raised by critics concerns how we

come to know a transcendent God. If God is beyond our human understanding, then there must be a source which reveals God's will to us. Without this source, we would have no true knowledge about God. This privileged source, be it the church, the Bible, or a religious leader, must convey without corruption the intentions of the transcendent God for the world. This model of the relationship between God and humanity stands or falls on whether this source is accorded that exalted status. If no such source exists, this model is unworkable. But what is this privileged source which is without error? Consensus on that source would be difficult to achieve. Second, if we limit the means through which the transcendent God can reveal to us, are we ourselves placing limits on God? By limiting God's revelation to an established means, are we discounting an important source of divine intervention? Isn't human life, apart from the usual religious practices, fertile ground for encountering God?

Those who emphasize God's transcendence are not without challenges of their own. The first deals with the process by which God's will is discerned, the second focuses attention on the distinction between the sacred and the secular.

Those who emphasize God's immanence see the religious life as consisting in following the deepest longings of our hearts since it is in the depths of the self that we encounter God. Critics ask, "How do we differentiate God's will from our own self-interest? Where do my longings end and God's will begin?" This problem of discernment has occupied a prominent place in the writings of the spiritual writers throughout Christian history. One must discern the spirit of God from one's own self-interest. But what degree of assurance can we have that we can successfully complete that task? The danger exists that we could pursue our own projects while at the same time claiming that we are following God's will. This might happen, for example, during times of war. Christians might raise the banner of their nation in the cause of a perceived holy war. If a cause or movement gives direction, purpose, and meaning to a person's life, does this make the movement legitimate in the eyes of God? Have not Christians at times had God underwrite their causes so that they could justify their actions? The transcendence model guards against this by raising up an objective standard to which we must conform. This standard prevents people from claiming divine authorization for their personal aspirations.

The second question raised by critics concerns the traditional distinction between the sacred and the secular, between the holy and the ordinary. Those who emphasize God's immanence contend that God's presence permeates all of human experience; we do not isolate one particular mode by which we experience it. All of human life is a valid means for experiencing God. Again this presents an appealing picture of all of creation speaking of the glory of the creator, but opponents ask whether this blurs the necessary distinction between the sacred and the secular. The transcendence model insists on the importance of this distinction. God has chosen certain channels to be the means of revelation to the world. For example, some may argue that the Bible is the word of God to the world. It is unlike any other book since God directly inspired its authors. Where the transcendence model restricts God's revelation an immanence model looks upon all things as possible channels for God's presence. Does this carry things too far? Is there a wisdom in preserving some distinction between the sacred and the secular? Should certain texts or practices be valued more than others? The immanence model seems less able than the transcendence model to offer a rationale for the reverence of certain texts and practices.

The dilemma of emphasizing either God's transcendence or immanence centers on which image of God one finds most compelling: the sovereign majestic God who created and sustains the universe and to whom we owe complete obedience or the creative Spirit moving through all creation which invites us to participate in the fullness of life. This dilemma is complicated, of course, by the fact that Christians maintain that both are true. Many Christians, in fact, draw upon the creative tension between these two portraits of God's presence to nourish their spiritual lives.

DISCUSSION QUESTIONS

1. Do you think of God primarily as transcendent or immanent?
2. Is there any feature of the other emphasis which you find appealing?
3. Which term do you prefer to describe the Christian life: obedience or cooperation?
4. Is there any feature of your portrait of God which you feel is subject to valid criticism?
5. Is there an image of God which combines both the transcendence and immanence of God?

SUGGESTED READING

Works by two of this century's leading Protestant theologians, H. Richard Niebuhr and Rudolf Bultmann, provide fine examples of theologies based in an understanding of God as transcendent. See H. Richard Niebuhr's *Radical Monotheism and Western Culture* (New York: Harper & Row, 1943) and the selection "Concerning the Hidden and Revealed God" in *Rudolf Bultmann: Interpreting Faith for the Modern Era* (London: Collins Liturgical Publications,

1987), edited by Roger Johnson. Johnson has a fine summary of this theme in Bultmann's work on pp. 18–21 of that volume.

For those with a greater familiarity with Protestant thought, Karl Barth's *The Humanity of God* (Atlanta: John Knox Press, 1960) is another fine example of this approach in theology.

For works written in a popular style based in an understanding of God as immanent, see Denis Edwards' *Human Experience of God* (Ramsey: Paulist, 1983) and Kenneth R. Overberg, S.J.'s *Roots and Branches: Grounding Religion in Our Human Experience* (Cincinnati: St. Anthony Messenger Press, 1988).

The Dilemma of Salvation
and Human Goodness

Do we need Christ or can we save ourselves?

"God did not send the Son into the world to condemn the world, but that the world might be saved through him" (Jn 3:17). There seems no more central affirmation of the Christian faith: Jesus Christ is the savior of the world. But what exactly does this mean? We save people from drowning; we save them from burning buildings. The act of saving consists of one person in danger and another person freeing that person from a perilous situation. The meaning of the expression "Jesus saves" is therefore to be found in an examination of two sets of questions. The first set involves the party being saved (i.e. humanity). Here we would ask, "Why do we need to be saved?" "How able is humanity to remedy its problem?" The second set of questions concerns the one doing the saving (i.e. Christ). Here we would like to know, "How does Christ free us from our situation?" and "In what does salvation consist? Eternal life? Happiness? Peace?" The meaning of "Jesus saves" lies in the correlation of the answers to those two sets of questions. This dilemma requires carefully balancing the fundamental problem of humanity with the solution offered by Christ. As we will see, the worse the situation, the greater the need for a savior. On the other hand, if the situation is not so dire, the need for a savior is diminished.

Jonathan Edwards, the fiery colonial revivalist, saw clearly the direct relationship between sin and salvation. In his famous "Sinners in the Hands of an Angry God" Edwards summons his congregation with great homiletic skill to a recognition of their wretched state as they teeter on the brink of eternal damnation. Edwards begins by describing in great detail the precarious state of those who have not been "born again." These uncon- verted "natural men" who are in an "unregenerate state" are "wicked." Because of their sinfulness, God should condemn this lot to the fires of hell. "There is nothing that keeps wicked men at any one moment out of hell, but the mere pleasure of God." The fate of the wicked is clear. "The wrath of God burns against them, their damnation does not slumber: the pit is pre- pared, the fire made ready, the furnace is now hot, ready to receive them; the flames do now rage and glow." The wicked person is like a man who walks over a pit on a rotten covering or a spider being held above the flame of a fire—each is ready at any moment to be destroyed.

Edwards correlates this pessimistic view of humanity with the great favor God has shown us in sending Christ into the world. Edwards declares,

> O Sinner! Consider the fearful danger you are in: it is a great furnace of wrath, a wide and bottomless pit, full of the fire of wrath, that you are held over in the hand of that God, whose wrath is provoked and incensed as much against you, as against many of the damned in hell. You hang by a slender thread, with the flames of divine wrath flashing about it, and ready every mo- ment to singe it, and burn it asunder; and you have no interest in any Mediator, and nothing to lay hold of to save yourself, nothing to keep off the flames of wrath, nothing of your own, nothing that you ever have done, nothing that you can do, to induce God to spare you one moment.

This passage from Edwards' sermon indicates the necessary connection between sin and salvation. Because of our sinfulness, we as humans are (a) in desperate need of salvation and (b) completely incapable of saving ourselves. Only Christ the mediator can save us from the flames of God's wrath. Despite his belief in predestination, Edwards maintains that people can recognize their sinfulness and throw themselves on the mercy of God and "obtain salvation." He preaches, "And now you have an extraordinary opportunity, a day wherein Christ has thrown the door of mercy wide open, and stands in calling and crying with a loud voice to poor sinners; a day wherein many are flocking to him, and pressing into the kingdom of God." Christ has provided us with an opportunity for salvation which we as humans could never achieve on our own.

For Edwards, salvation consists in freedom from eternal damnation. Edwards graphically paints a picture of the misery which those in hell suffer. They are subject to the unrelenting wrath of God in all its fierceness. For all eternity those in hell will suffer the torment of the vengeance of God. "If you cry to God to pity you, he will be so far from pitying you in your doleful case, or showing you the least regard of favour, that instead of that, he will only tread you under foot. And though he will know that you cannot bear the weight of omnipotence treading upon you, yet he will not regard that, but he will crush you under his feet without mercy; he will crush out your blood, and make it fly, and it shall be sprinkled on his garments. . . ." The meaning of salvation is therefore unambiguously clear. The fundamental problem of humanity is sinfulness which merits eternal damnation. Christ, however, throws open the door of mercy and through that door we will enjoy eternal bliss in heaven.

The relationship between sinfulness and salvation is clearly defined in Edwards' sermon. Edwards exalted Christ and denigrated humanity. What becomes of salvation, however, for those who do not share Edwards' estimation of humanity? What if humans are not seen as wretched? What if the fundamental problem is not sinfulness? Norman Vincent Peale, the great proponent of positive thinking, offers a much different analysis of the human condition than that presented by Jonathan Edwards. For Peale, and many others, the fundamental problem is not that humans fail to recognize their wretchedness, but rather that they fail to recognize their goodness. The problem is not egocentric pride; it is a lack of self-appreciation.

In his famous work *The Power of Positive Thinking* Peale writes, "Lack of self-confidence apparently is one of the great problems besetting people today.... Everywhere you encounter people who are inwardly afraid, who shrink from life, who suffer from a deep sense of inadequacy and insecurity, who doubt their own powers. Deep within themselves they mistrust their abilities to meet responsibilities or to grasp opportunities." The picture presented by Peale relies a great deal on his psychological research. He maintains that experiences in our youth directly affect our self-image. Too often that influence is negative and people are plagued by feelings of doubt and a general lack of self confidence. This "inferiority complex" prevents genuine human fulfillment—the very fulfillment which God has created us to enjoy. This malady permeates our entire existence, from our interpersonal relationships to our business dealings.

The solution to this "inferiority complex" is both psychological and theological. Peale offers such practical advice, e.g., repeating positive sayings each morning, listing the positive things in one's life on a sheet of paper, and creating a mental picture of oneself as successful. These exercises are rooted not only in good psychology, but good theology as well, according to Peale. "The greatest secret for eliminating the inferiority complex, which is another term for deep and profound self-doubt, is to fill your mind to overflowing with faith. Develop a tremendous faith in God and that will give you a humble, yet soundly realistic faith in yourself." This joining of faith in God with faith in oneself is fundamental to Peale's thought. "One of

the most powerful concepts, one which is a sure cure for lack of
confidence, is the thought that God is actually with you and
helping you." Peale places particular emphasis on those biblical verses which speak of courage and confidence. He lists
among his favorites: "I can do all things through Christ which
strengtheneth me" (Phil 4:13), "If ye have faith . . . nothing
shall be impossible unto you" (Mt 17:20), and "If God be for us,
who can be against us?" (Rom 8:31).

The theological question which arises at this point concerns the role Christ plays in this scheme. For Edwards, Christ's
role was so desperately needed because of the horrible condition of humanity. When humanity is viewed in far more optimistic terms, what becomes of Christ? The greater the ability of
humans to raise themselves up out of their condition, the less
they need a savior. In the following passage, Peale describes
the beliefs shared by the psychiatrists and ministers on staff at
his church.

> We believe in the practical, absolute workability of
> the teachings of Jesus. We believe that we can indeed
> "do all things through Christ." (Philippians 4:13) The
> Gospel as we work with it proves to be a literal fulfill-
> ment of the astonishing promise, "Eye hath not seen,
> nor ear heard, neither have entered into the heart of
> man, the things which God hath prepared for them
> that love Him." (1 Corinthians 2:9) Believe (in Christ);
> believe in His system of thought and practice; believe
> and you will overcome all fear, hate, inferiority, guilt,
> and every form and manner of defeat. In other words,
> no good thing is too good to be true. You have never
> seen, never heard, never even imagined the things
> God will give to those who love Him.

Through belief in Christ's "system," we are able to overcome all
of those things which defeat us. What becomes of Christ? If we

are capable of solving our inferiority complexes, what need do we have of a savior?

Here then we see the dilemma. What becomes of Christ's role as Savior when we no longer hold that humans are essentially wretched or that our dominant concern is the avoidance of eternal damnation? Can we maintain a belief in the essential goodness of humanity without undercutting the relevance of Christ for humanity?

It might help at this point to introduce two related discussions of the problem of the human condition. The first deals with the "deprived/depraved" distinction and the second focuses on the Adam and Eve story. The first shorthand method asks, "Are humans deprived or depraved?" Both terms attempt to explain the very observable fact of human sinfulness. Do humans act sinfully because they simply lack the proper upbringing? Or is the problem more severe? Is the tendency toward sin rooted in our very nature? If this tendency is overpowering, then humans are said to be depraved. Here again we walk a tightrope. On the one hand, if we argue that humans are deprived, we may not give sufficient attention to the horrible suffering humans have caused down through the ages. On the other hand, if we argue that humans are depraved, we may neglect to give sufficient attention to the tremendous acts of kindness and selflessness that humans have performed for their neighbors. The second shorthand method of discussing this question is more theological. It involves the story of Adam and Eve and their fall from paradise. While not a literal tale of human origins, the garden of Eden story presents a view of humanity which has dominated Christian thought down through the centuries. The question parallels the deprived/depraved debate. Is the story of the fall to be seen as describing an act of a pair of children who are beginning a rather lengthy process of moral growth or an adult act of deliberate disobedience and rebellion against God? The story supports both interpretations.

The former, the "mild" interpretation of the fall, would argue that humans are deprived. The latter, the "harsh" interpretation of the fall, would argue that humans are depraved. Any assessment of humanity must recognize the pettiness, jealousy, and hatred which lurks within our hearts as well as the kindness, mercy, and love which we extend to others.

Many contemporary theologians have attempted to maintain a more optimistic view of humanity while at the same time preserving the importance of Christ as the savior of the world. Before concluding our discussion, we will briefly review two approaches which cast the issue of salvation in a different light. The first will be labeled the "relational approach," the second will be labeled "the political approach." The degree to which these reformulations are successful is dependent on the severity of the problem which Jesus solves.

In the relational approach, Jesus is our savior in that he saved us from false notions about God, neighbor, and self, thus enabling us to enter into a relationship with all three which is constructive and healthy. Those who advance this type of argument rightly point out that the root of the word salvation is *salus* which means health or well-being. In this psychological perspective Christ frees us from our destructive and misguided notions about God, others, and self. Our fears cause us to look upon God as a judge who stands over us waiting to condemn us, our neighbors as strangers who threaten us and ourselves as sinners who are unworthy of God's love. In this condition, we resist God because God is seen as an implacable overlord. We act with resentment and violence toward others and we concentrate on our failures and shortcomings. Christ, however, brings a message of love which enables us to experience the love of the Father, the solidarity of human fellowship, and the goodness of our own selves. Salvation consists then in being freed from those constraints which hinder our development as God's sons and daughters in communion with all of the human race. Jesus saves us from the threefold alienation from God, neighbor, and self. Without Jesus, we are "damned" to a life of fear, isolation, and insecurity.

The political approach is often associated with a movement known as "liberation theology." The fundamental problem confronting humans is the perpetuation of poverty and injustice. This condition produces a host of ills ranging from illiteracy to government-sanctioned violence. The liberation theologians argue that salvation has become a "spiritual" concept unrelated to the ordinary practical concerns of day to day living. Salvation must not be seen apart from the legitimate concerns for clean water, decent housing, proper health care, and education. To separate those two realms of our existence in that way, contend the liberation theologians, amounts to saying that God is concerned only with our soul and not with our body. Jesus taught us not only to pray, but also to feed the hungry, give drink to the thirsty, clothe the naked, comfort the ill, and visit the imprisoned. Salvation in this second approach is the release of the oppressed. The poor are oppressed by their poverty; the wealthy are oppressed by their riches. In order to restore well-being to the world, we need to create just economic and political systems. Working toward that goal is an act of salvation—it saves people from needless suffering. Eternal life continues to comprise a good deal of what it means to be saved, but the process of salvation begins in this life.

These two alternative views of salvation, the relational and the political, represent attempts to move away from the notion that humans are wicked and salvation is entrance into heaven. Three important questions remain. First, the two approaches certainly provide meaningful insights into the gospel; however, do those insights come uniquely from Jesus' preaching? Could these insights be learned elsewhere? Could we learn the same insights from one of the great philosophers, poets, founders of world religions, or even by an examination of our life experience? If these insights could be gathered from these other sources, does that diminish Christ's role as savior? Second, are we now manipulating Jesus? Are we defining our problem and then fitting Jesus into our scheme? Even if such a project is not necessarily misguided, are there dangers that we are making up our own version of the gospel? Third, are we dealing adequately with the significance of the cross? The saving act of Christ traditionally has been linked with his crucifixion. "In his own body he brought your sins to the cross, so that all of us, dead to sin, could live in accord with God's will. By his wounds you were healed" (1 Pet 2:24). "It pleased God to make absolute fullness reside in him and, by means of him, to reconcile everything in his person, both on earth and in the heavens, making peace through the blood of his cross (Col 1:19–20). The scriptures are filled with such references: Christ gave his life as a ransom for the many (Mk 10:45), Christ gave himself for us as an offering to God (Eph 5:2), Christ died for us and we have been justified by his blood (Rom 5:8–9). If the cross does not play a prominent or decisive role in our view of salvation, is it a faithful re-presentation of the gospel message?

This dilemma is rooted in the very language of salvation. Language of this nature requires that humans be in some type of peril from which they are unable to rescue themselves. If humans are seen as damned because of their wickedness, then salvation is the availability of eternal life in heaven through the cross of Christ. If humans are not essentially wicked or if the fundamental problem is present meaninglessness rather than eternal damnation, then a tension arises over the role of Christ as the unique bearer of salvation for all the world. The dilemma remains: Can we affirm simultaneously the goodness of humanity, the uniqueness of Christ as savior, and the significance of Christ's crucifixion as the means through which we are saved?

DISCUSSION QUESTIONS

1. From what does Christ save us? How able are we to save ourselves?
2. In your estimation, how sinful is humanity?
3. Is salvation strictly a religious concept? Can we apply salvation to questions of political involvement?
4. Do you believe in hell? Why or why not?

SUGGESTED READING

Denis Edwards' *What Are They Saying About Salvation?* (Mahwah: Paulist Press, 1986) is an excellent review of the "state of the question."

Gerald O'Collins offers a fine summary of the biblical material on salvation in Chapter Five of his *Interpreting Jesus* (Ramsey: Paulist, 1983).

Donald Gray offers a different perspective on the saving work of Jesus in Chapter One of his *Jesus: The Way to Freedom* (Winona: St. Mary's Press, 1979).

The articles "Salvation" in the *New Catholic Encyclopedia* (New York: McGraw Hill, 1967) and "Atonement" in the *Encyclopedia of Religion* (New York: Macmillan, 1987) are helpful, brief summaries.

A political perspective on salvation can be found in Chapter

Nine of Gustavo Gutierrez's *A Theology of Liberation* (Maryknoll: Orbis, 1973).

The advanced theological student would benefit from John Hicks' discussion of the two dominant interpretations of the fall in his *Evil and the God of Love* (New York: Harper & Row, 1978) and Karl Rahner's article on "Salvation" in the *Encyclopedia of Theology: The Concise Sacramentum Mundi* (New York: Crossroad, 1975).

The Dilemma of Evil

Why does God let innocent people suffer?

The events reported in the daily newspapers often pose what might well be the most troublesome of all theological dilemmas. The dilemma arises from the fact that Christians believe in an all-knowing, all-loving, and all-powerful God, yet live in a world in which freak accidents, natural disasters, and acts of violence against defenseless victims are not uncommon. Can these two realities be reconciled? Believers insist that they can. Others, however, offer the following argument:

(1) Christians believe in an all-knowing, all-loving, and all-powerful God.

(2) An all-knowing God should know how to create a world without evil; an all-loving God should want to create such a world; and an all-powerful God should have the ability to create such a world.

(3) Evil exists in the world.

(4) Therefore, an all-knowing, all-loving, and all-powerful God does not exist.

This argument provides the framework for our exploration of the various responses to the problem of evil.

Christians who wish to respond to the argument above must attack the truth of one or more of its premises. In theological terminology this attempt is known as a "theodicy," a term derived from the Greek words for "God" and "justice." A theodicy affirms God's justice despite the presence of evil and suffering in the world. The first set of responses to the problem of evil which we will consider centers on the first premise: Christians believe in an all-knowing, all-loving, and all-powerful God.

Dualism is the belief that the universe is not controlled by one power, but by two. In dualistic thought, God is not all-powerful; rather, God's power is limited by some other force. This dualistic thought takes one of two forms. The first we will label "permanent dualism" and the second "temporary dualism." In "permanent dualism," the universe *has always and will always* be torn between the forces of light and darkness. In certain ancient mythologies, for example, a god representing the power of goodness and a god representing the power of evil are involved in a relentless seesaw battle for control of human affairs. In "temporary dualism," there is an independent evil force at work in the world at *the present time.* This evil force, however, will not always exist as a rival to God. Nor will it exist for all eternity. God will ultimately banish all evil from the world. The belief in a devil who works in opposition to the will of God represents this type of dualistic thought. For a time the devil will cause havoc in the world, but the devil's activity will one day cease.

Proponents assert that both forms of dualism offer reasonable responses to the problem of evil. First, both provide a ready explanation for any misfortune which should befall a person—namely, the person fell victim to the activity of the forces which oppose God's will. In everyday speech, for example, we refer to a person experiencing "bad luck." Since God is not all-powerful, God is no longer held responsible for the evils which occur in the world. A second argument advanced by advocates of both types of dualism contends that evil must exist so that we may come to know the meaning of goodness. They argue that we come to understand the meaning of concepts only by experiencing their opposites. For example, we can

know the meaning of "sweet" only by comparing it to something that is "sour." Evil, therefore, serves as a necessary foil to
the goodness in the world.

The response of the theological community to dualistic
thought has been mixed. Some theologians have willingly
surrendered the belief that God is all-powerful. They contend
that while God cannot prevent evil from occurring, God is present as a source of comfort and support for those who have
experienced the effects of evil. God suffers along with the person who has been affected or afflicted by evil. Despite acceptance in some quarters in the theological community, these
dualistic solutions are far from universally accepted. Most
Christian theologians have rejected "permanent dualism" on
the basis that it surrenders what they consider to be the indispensable belief that God is all-powerful. They charge that any
restrictions on God's power (other than those God would freely
choose) compromise God's status as the almighty, supreme
power in the universe. The "temporary dualism" position has
traditionally received a more favorable review from Christian
theologians, but it too faces a challenge. Critics ask, "Where did
evil originate?" Recall, for example, the mythical story of the
garden of Eden. In the midst of this garden paradise there
crawled the tempter. How did this force of instability enter
paradise? Did God create a world which was less than perfect?
If so, ask the critics, is God responsible for the evil in the world?
The same questions could be applied to the mythical story of
the fallen angels who rebelled against God. Why would angelic
beings rebel against their creator? The traditional response is
that they were endowed with free will by their creator and they
chose to disobey God. It is to this solution to the problem that
we now turn.

The second set of responses to the problem of evil deals
with the second premise: An all-knowing God should know
how to create a world without evil; an all-loving God should

want to create such a world; and an all-powerful God should have the ability to create such a world. Many Christian theologians have argued against this premise. The common thread which runs throughout their diverse arguments is that the presence of evil does not in itself negate the fact that God is all-knowing, all-loving, or all-powerful.

The "free will defense" offers a case for the existence of evil in a world created by an all-knowing, all-loving, all-powerful God. The argument is simple: evil exists because humans improperly use their free will. In this view, God created "the best of all possible worlds" by creating a world in which genuine human freedom exists. God could have created a world in which neither evil nor human freedom existed, but that world would not be as good as a world with genuine free will and the unfortunate reality of evil resulting from this freedom. The evils which can occur in this world are, as we all know, horrible indeed. When terrorists choose to plant a bomb on board an airliner, their choices result in the death of hundreds of innocent passengers. When unscrupulous individuals choose to defraud investors, their actions result in human hardship. The free will defense does not place the blame on God, but rather on those who use their freedom in a destructive way. God is not responsible for the moral evil in the world—humans alone bear responsibility for their actions.

The free will defense is not without its critics. One of the more popular criticisms is that God could have created a world in which persons possess genuine human freedom, yet always choose to do the good. Critics charge that this imaginary world would be "the best of all possible worlds." Second, even if the free will defense offers a cogent account of how much of the evil in the world arises, the argument does not deal with the evil which results from causes other than human freedom. Earthquakes, hurricanes, and tidal waves (so-called "acts of God") also cause human suffering, but these are not caused by human choice. Theologians label the evil which results from human activity "moral" evil and the evil which results from non-human activity "physical" or "natural" evil. Some theologians contend that natural evil is an unfortunate by-product of the workings of an extremely complex global ecosystem. The very elements which sustain life throughout the world (e.g. air, water, sunlight) often create conditions or events which destroy human life. The development and movement of a hurricane, for example, depends on a host of factors: water temperature, air temperature, jet stream patterns, etc. These elements are also responsible for a number of atmospheric conditions which make human life more enjoyable. Critics question why God did not create a world with a better ecosystem, one which did not so frequently destroy human life. They also ask why certain individuals are killed and others are not. Why doesn't God intervene to save the innocent when these natural disasters arise?

It might be helpful to recall the premise of the argument under consideration: An all-knowing God should know how to create a world without evil; an all-loving God should want to create such a world; and an all-powerful God should have the ability to create such a world. As mentioned above, the free will argument responds to those who say that evil is incompatible with an all-knowing, all-powerful God. The free will defense does not deal directly with the problem of natural evil. That issue is addressed more directly by those who wish to preserve the compatibility between an all-loving God and the reality of evil in the world.

The first argument which attempts to reconcile God's love with the presence of evil in the world offers an alternative interpretation of the fall from paradise in Genesis 3. This mythical story has been of lasting importance to the discussion of the problem of evil. Christians have traditionally derived two important themes from this story. The first is that God originally created the universe in harmony. The second is that humans misused their gift of freedom and brought disharmony into the world. As discussed in the previous chapter on salvation and human goodness, the story of the fall has been understood by some theologians as a statement of human depravity. Those who wish to reconcile God's love with the presence of evil offer a different interpretation of this classic story. They look upon the fall as the initial phase of a long process of evolutionary growth. In this view, pain and suffering need not be incompatible with a loving God.

Human life is filled with abundant examples of the coexistence of positive or benevolent action and human suffering. For example, athletes must undergo strenuous programs of physical training in order to better their performance. In order to cure a patient a doctor must often prescribe a treatment which initially causes the patient greater discomfort. A loving parent may on occasion not prevent a child from experiencing either physical or emotional pain in the hope that such an experience will prove instructive or valuable in some way. Using examples such as these, some have argued for the compatibility of a loving God and human suffering. The argument works in two ways. The first focuses attention on the suffering experienced by an individual over the course of his or her life; the second focuses attention on the suffering experienced by humanity over the course of human history. In the first view, an individual struggles and falls, succeeds and fails, in his or her journey toward moral goodness. The failings result in evil, but the successes result in tested virtue. In the second view, a developmental view of humanity allows for collective suffering and an all-loving God. Additionally, the presence of physical evil can as well be seen as part of an obstacle course which humans, both individually and collectively, encounter as they grow in wisdom and goodness.

This developmental perspective seeks to reconcile belief in a loving God with the reality of evil. Critics, however, are quick to attack this approach to the problem of evil. The first criticism concerns the manner of distribution of evil in the world. Some suffer a great deal, others very little. Critics ask, "If suffering is a necessary part of human formation, why is there such a radical disparity in the amount of suffering people must endure?" The second criticism concerns the seeming senselessness of much of human suffering. It is true that human failing is often an occasion for insight and conversion; however, not all human suffering seems to serve this useful purpose. Critics ask, "What possible value could prisoners of conscience derive from the horrible experience of torture and execution?"

The second attempt to reconcile God's goodness with the presence of human suffering is one of the most ancient solutions: human suffering is a punishment from God. The Bible contains countless examples of divine punishment. The book of Judges, for example, is filled with verses such as this: "The Israelites again offended the Lord, who therefore delivered them into the power of the Philistines for forty years" (13:1). Interestingly, the experience of the covenant people called this explanation into question. Faithful followers of God discovered that the wicked often prospered, while the just often suffered. The sober tone of the book of Ecclesiastes betrays the mood of the author who questions whether justice truly exists: "This is a vanity which occurs on earth: there are just men treated as though they had done evil and wicked men treated as though they had done justly. This, too, I say is vanity" (8:14). The book of Job which we discussed in the earlier chapter on God's presence deals explicitly with the problem of the suffering of the innocent. In the New Testament Jesus himself seems to reject the simple equation of sin with divine retribution. In Luke's gospel, we find the following account:

> At that time, some were present who told him about
> the Galileans whose blood Pilate had mixed with their

sacrifices. He said in reply: "Do you think that these Galileans were the greatest sinners in Galilee just because they suffered this? By no means! But I tell you, you will all come to the same end unless you reform. Or take those eighteen who were killed by a falling tower in Siloam. Do you think they were more guilty than anyone else who lived in Jerusalem? Certainly not! But I tell you, you will all come to the same end unless you reform" (13:1–5).

The claim that a person's suffering is proportionate to a person's sin has, in the eyes of many of the faithful down through the centuries, proven to be an inaccurate assessment of how God works in the world.

The third attempt to reconcile God's goodness with the presence of evil frequently draws upon the analogy of fine art or music. A composer, for example, arranges notes in a specific order in order to produce a melodic musical piece. Heard in isolation, certain notes sound discordant; however, when placed properly in a movement they contribute to the grace and beauty of the composition. In the same way, what may appear to be evil to the human eye might actually be a small part of God's overall scheme. Critics charge that the portrait of God presumed in this position is unappealing. God would be allowing millions of people to suffer simply to serve as a contrast to other people's pleasure.

The starting point of the fourth attempt to reconcile God's goodness with human suffering is a claim about human nature. Humans, it is argued, are largely concerned with their own affairs. This basic egocentricity leads to a distorted view of the world. We view the events of the world in terms of the impact these events have on our own lives. The self displaces God as the center of our world. The natural aging process and human suffering, however, serve as powerful reminders that our time on earth is limited and our energies need to be spent in the services of God and neighbor. Critics again ask whether this solution properly accounts for the quantity of evil in the world. Is the amount of evil in the world necessary to achieve the goal of shattering the egocentric illusions of humanity?

The next set of responses to the problem of evil centers attention on the third premise: Evil exists. This would seem an unlikely premise to attack since life provides ample evidence for the existence of evil. Of the various attempts to deny the existence of evil, only one will be examined. This position does not deny that evil exists, but it does deny that evil exists as an independent power. Evil, in this view, is the absence of good. To cite an ancient example, we do not look upon the fact that humans lack wings as evil. We would, however, not make the same claim about a bird which lacked a wing. Because something was lacking which should have been there, we would call the latter example a case of evil. If we take this insight as the key to understanding evil, evil is not a power existing in its own right; it is the deprivation of a good. Critics charge that while this response may offer an interesting perspective on the nature of evil, it does not seem to offer much comfort to those who are suffering. To label disease a lack of health is correct, but it leaves unanswered the question asked by many of those afflicted with terminal illness, "Why me?"

Some find this premise by premise discussion of the problem of evil misguided. For them the problem of evil is an impenetrable mystery. Like Job we must simply trust in the Lord. Others insist that only in the afterlife will all things be made right: those who were wicked will be punished and those who were just will be rewarded. For others the problem of evil must be viewed in light of the great mystery of Christ's suffering, death, and resurrection. In this view, Christ's cross is the means by which God will restore all of creation and Christians must trust that this plan will indeed be carried out in the fullness of time.

A formal discussion of the problem of evil certainly does not begin to capture the anguish of those who have suffered great tragedy in their lives. Nor does it settle the question once and for all. It does, however, provide Christians an opportunity to reflect on the relationship between God and humanity. Yet as long as we encounter the senseless violence against the elderly, the death of children and the human devastation caused by drought and famine we will continue to struggle to resolve this most perplexing of theological dilemmas.

DISCUSSION QUESTIONS

1. Which solution, if any, do you find most satisfying? Which solution do you find least satisfying?
2. Are there any responses to the problem of evil not included in this chapter which you find appealing?
3. What percentage of the world's problems are a result of the misuse of human freedom?
4. Is the claim that the problem of evil is a mystery which humans will never resolve an avoidance of the question or a legitimate response?

SUGGESTED READING

An extremely helpful introduction to this problem is *What Are They Saying About God and Evil?* by Barry L. Whitney (Mahwah: Paulist Press, 1989).

The entries "Evil, The Problem of" and "Theodicy" in *The Westminster Dictionary of Christian Theology* (Philadelphia: Westminster Press, 1983) are short, but helpful.

Harold Kushner's *When Bad Things Happen to Good People* (New York: Schocken Books, 1981) was widely read. Most introductory texts to the philosophy of religion devote space to the problem of evil.

Advanced theological students should consult the bibliography at the end of the Whitney text for further readings. John Hicks' entry "Evil, the Problem of" in the *Encyclopedia of Philosophy* (New York: Macmillan, 1967) as well as his *Evil and the God of Love* (San Francisco: Harper & Row, 1966, revised edition 1978) are informative.

Diogenes Allen addresses the problem of evil in a number of his writings. See his *The Traces of God in a Frequently Hostile World* (Cambridge: Cowley Publications, 1981).

The Dilemma of Christianity and the Other World Religions

Is Christianity the only true religion?

Is Christianity the only true religion? On the one hand, it would seem that either Christianity is right and all other religions are wrong or vice versa. After all, Christianity is based on two claims: There is one God and Jesus is God's definitive revealer. To argue that there is not one God (as, for example, is the case in Hinduism) or that Jesus is not the most important of God's messengers (as, for example, is the case in Islam) is to make a claim which is simply incompatible with Christianity. There is either one God or many gods. Either Christ is God's definitive revealer or he is not. Both claims cannot be true. In this view, truth is the "exclusive" property of one religion. On the other hand, many find the idea that truth is found exclusively in Christianity nothing more than a display of arrogance. They maintain that saying other religions are true only to the extent that they agree with what Christians believe is nonsense. Different cultures manifest the contact with the divine in different ways. In this "inclusive" view, the various world religions are simply different paths to the same reality and can all rightfully be called true. In this chapter we will examine the logic of these two responses to the question, "Is Christianity the only true religion?" This dilemma asks Christians to balance their reverence for Christ as God's Son with an appreciation of other forms of religious expression.

Advocates of the "exclusive" position argue that numerous biblical texts present Christ as God's exclusive agent of salvation. The following four verses are often cited in support of this claim. In John's gospel, Jesus says, "I am the way, and the truth, and the life; no one comes to the Father but through me" (14:6). In Acts, Peter proclaims, "This Jesus is 'the stone rejected by you the builders which has become the cornerstone.' There is no salvation in anyone else, for there is no other name in the whole world given to men by which they are to be saved" (4:11–12). In his letter to the Romans, Paul declares, "For if you confess with your lips that Jesus is Lord, and believe in your heart that God raised him from the dead, you will be saved. Faith in the heart leads to justification, confession on the lips to salvation" (10:9–10). Lastly, the author of 1 Timothy writes, "And the truth is this: God is one. One also is the mediator between God and men, the man Christ Jesus, who gave himself as a ransom for all" (2:5). Proponents of the exclusive position insist that Christianity stands or falls on the truth of these scriptural claims about Jesus. If Christ is not the one mediator between God and humanity, then Christianity is wrong. If Christ is the one mediator, then Christianity is right. The scriptural texts demand that we make a choice between belief in one God or many gods and between one mediator or many mediators.

Those in this exclusive school of thought contend that the exaltation of Christ above all other beings is an indispensable affirmation of the Christian faith; to surrender that claim is to abandon the faith. The earlier discussion of high and low christology reappears here. The logic of a high christology is that Jesus is God's only Son. The "higher" the christology, therefore, the less significance one attaches to religious figures other than Jesus. If Christianity is not the one true religion, then Christ is equal in importance to the founders of Buddhism, Islam, or Taoism. Christ would be one of many leaders of great insight revered by religious believers.

Those who advocate the "inclusive" position feel it is simply ludicrous for members of one religion to claim that their religion is the only avenue by which the divine is to be found. Humans around the world have gained valuable insights into the nature of the great force which sustains the universe ("God," "Ultimate Reality," "the One," etc.). They are, as an ancient proverb suggests, similar to a group of people examining an elephant in the dark. One person describes the elephant's long trunk, another the tail, and a third the feet. All report different aspects of the same reality. Gifted individuals in various cultures have offered profound responses to the questions of ultimate significance for human life (e.g. what is the meaning of life? what is a "life well lived"? what things are of greatest value?). They have in turn shared their discoveries with others on the journey toward truth. Their ideas were so enlightening and so powerful that others committed themselves to living according to their teachings. At their root, all the great religious traditions are based on the insights of a person or group of persons who saw more clearly the answers to the questions we ourselves are asking.

Proponents of this inclusive position argue that their opponents are ignoring an entire world of religious insight by seeking truth in a single religion. Once we surrender our mistaken notion that we alone possess the truth, we can then learn the lessons which the other religions have to teach us. This process offers two benefits. The first is that the other religions challenge some of our fundamental ideas about the nature of reality. In this way, we can break out of the confines of our limited worldview. The teachings of Taoism, for example, stress a oneness with nature and an acceptance of the joy and pain of human existence. The second benefit is the expansion and enrichment of one's own spirituality. For example, an exploration of Buddhist meditative practices could help us develop a deeper prayer life as Christians. Our willingness to learn from those in other traditions is dependent upon our respect and willingness to find a truth there which may not be present in Christianity.

The inclusive approach looks upon all religious traditions as "truthful." This approach, contend its advocates, offers a number of advantages. The first and most obvious advantage is that this perspective provides a rationale for interreligious dialogue. Christians could learn the truths taught by the Buddhists or Hindus and vice versa. Second, it extends the boundaries of where truth can be found. Not only does truth reside outside of Christianity, it resides outside explicit religious traditions. The writings of the great philosophers and poets also contain a wealth of insight into the great questions of human existence. Any source which enlightens us or enables us to create a more just society is a reservoir of truth. The final point is often raised as a question: Why would a just God restrict truth to one religious tradition and leave a large portion of the world's population in error? Isn't it imperialistic of Christians to say that other religious traditions are true only to the extent that they agree with their beliefs?

The inclusive position was popularized in the seventeenth and eighteenth centuries by a group of thinkers known as "deists." They argued, first of all, on political grounds that mutual toleration of one another's views was necessary to ensure the stability of society. Europe was recovering from the pain and devastation of the Thirty Years' War (1618–1648), a series of "religious wars" between Catholics and Protestants. The death toll was enormous. The exclusive position seemed to increase, rather than decrease, hostility and friction between competing religious groups. If social stability were to be achieved, there would need to be a platform upon which all parties could agree. Out of this concern grew deism or the "natural religion" movement. The natural religion consisted of a set of truths which all reasonable persons would accept as binding. There was no appeal to outside authorities such as the pope, the Bible, or church statements. Reason alone was sufficient. In contrast to the natural religion, "revealed religions" are based on the teachings of a "revealer." The knowledge imparted by the revealer is not available through reason, but rather must be taught to us. The principles of the natural religion, according to Lord Herbert of Cherbury (1583–1648), are (1) God exists, (2) God ought to be worshiped, (3) doing good deeds is the chief part of the worship of God, (4) people should repent of their sins, and (5) there are rewards and punishments after death.

The deists also argued for the inclusive position on theological grounds. The deist Matthew Tindal (1655–1733) contended that the exclusive position denied the fairness of God. In his *Christianity as Old as the Creation* he argues against the need for revealed religions. He begins with two claims: (1) God does not change and (2) human nature does not change. God has always been wise and good and always will be. Human nature as well does not change from generation to generation. Since God is all good, God would want all people to have knowledge of the true religion. Since people were no different two thousand years ago than they are today, people of past generations were no less capable of understanding the true religion. Therefore, if God is to be fair, God would have to give all people of all time equal access to knowledge of the true religion. Since this is the case, those living before Christ would not be at any disadvantage to those who lived after Christ. If God were to reveal certain things to specific people, but not to others, God would be unfair. Since not all people in the world encountered Christianity, it would be unjust of God to require belief in Christ as a condition for salvation. The truths of religion are to be found through the use of the reason which all humans possess and not in the teachings of a particular historical figure.

The question arose in the Enlightenment, "If our reason

provides us with the necessary knowledge for salvation, what need do we have for Jesus?" The thinkers of the Enlightenment could offer only practical answers. For example, Jesus summarized and presented in a clear, concise manner the truths which were discovered in fragmentary ways over the past centuries. Jesus taught this message with such power that its truth was clearly seen. They believed that although Jesus was a great preacher, he added no new content to the message. Others claimed that the revelation given to Moses was confined to a small portion of the world. Jesus, by contrast, taught in great urban areas where commerce and communication were developed to a far greater extent so that Jesus was able to spread the message more quickly to a greater number of people. Whatever role Jesus played, it was merely functional. Thinkers in the natural religion movement insisted that with sufficient rational reflection all persons could discover the "true religion." Any claim about being the only true religion was simply group-aggrandizement.

Both the exclusive and inclusive positions must address difficult questions. We will conclude this discussion by directing a question at each group. The exclusive position must deal with the question: Are non-Christians saved? The inclusive position must deal with the question: What constitutes a valid religion?

The exclusive position argues that God sent a savior, not saviors, into the world. Jesus Christ is God's exclusive agent of salvation. To depart from that truth is to deny the core of the Christian message. This raises an interesting related question: Does a person need to make an explicit confession of belief in Jesus in order to enter into eternal life? As we have seen, certain biblical verses suggest that indeed such a confession is necessary for salvation. Christian history is filled with thinkers who restricted salvation to a chosen few. Cyprian, an early church theologian, wrote, "He can no longer have God for his Father, who has not the Church for his mother." The principle was often succinctly stated: "Outside the church there is no salvation." Christ was the way to God, the church was the way to Christ, and baptism was the way into the church. Christ established the church as a lasting means through which people on earth could acquire the necessary grace in order to enter into everlasting life. Christ assigned the care of the church to Peter and his successors, and through their sacramental ministry members of the church were provided with an avenue for salvation. Separation from the church therefore endangered a person's eternal salvation. Others have claimed that only those who explicitly confess Jesus as Lord or who are "born again" (cf. Jn 3:3) can be saved. This raises some practical questions: Are the millions of non-Christians damned to hell? Are our Jewish neighbors or non-religious friends unable to enter into eternal life? Is Gandhi in hell? Are Christians who have not been "born again" able to go to heaven? The exclusive position does not necessarily dismiss the possibility of salvation for non-Christians. It can certainly be argued that Christ, as the exclusive agent of salvation, saves all persons, not just those who are baptized or those who are "born again." The question of the salvation of non-Christians or those who fail to meet some other criterion, however, remains an important question for those who advocate the exclusive position.

The inclusive position needs to address the difficult question: What constitutes a valid religion? Are all religions equally true? Are other movements which are not listed among the traditional world religions valid religions? Are the various cults in the country valid religions? The problem lies in defining what exactly qualifies as a religion. If all of those movements are regarded as equally valid religious expressions, then there seems to be no standard of validity. Any "religion" is just as good or true as any other "religion." If, on the other hand, certain movements are not "religions," then the standards by which those distinctions are drawn need to be specified and justified. It is the justification of those standards which will prove most difficult for the advocates of the inclusive position.

The dilemma arises from the tension between two legitimate interests. The first is the insistence on the truth of Christianity and the decisive importance of Jesus for the world. The second is an openness and appreciation of other religious traditions as sources of goodness, truth and beauty. As the American culture becomes more pluralistic and as contact with foreign countries increases, the urgency of this question intensifies. From questions of intermarriage to foreign policy, the understanding of the relationship of Christianity to the other world religions plays an important role in the discussion.

DISCUSSION QUESTIONS

1. Is Christianity the only true religion? State the reasons for your position. Anticipate your opponent's objections and respond to them.

2. Is Jesus *a* representative of God or *the* representative of God?

3. By what standards (if any) do we judge the truth and goodness of movements claiming to be religious movements?

4. What features of other religions do you find appealing?

SUGGESTED READING

The *Declaration on the Relationship of the Church to Non-Christian Religions*, contained in the standard collections of the Vatican II documents, presents the official Roman Catholic position.

What Are They Saying About Christ and World Religions? (Ramsey: Paulist Press, 1981) by Lucien Richard, O.M.I. is a clear and concise review of the major positions in the debate.

Chapter 11 of Kathleen R. Fischer and Thomas N. Hart's *Christian Foundations: An Introduction to Faith in Our Time* (Mahwah: Paulist Press, 1986) and pp. 267–277 of Richard McBrien's *Catholicism* (Minneapolis: Winston, 1980) are shorter discussions of the question.

The popular book *The Power of Myth* (New York: Doubleday, 1988) by Joseph Campbell with Bill Moyers argues for the presence of persistent themes in human cultures throughout the ages.

See also Leonard J. Biallas' *Myths, Gods, Heros, and Saviors* (Mystic: Twenty-Third Publications, 1986).

Advanced theological students would benefit from reading the editorial symposium on "Jesus' Unsurpassable Uniqueness" in *Horizons* 16(1), Spring 1989, 101–130.

The Dilemma of Dissent

Can we disagree with Church teaching and still be good Catholics?

Roman Catholics in the United States live in two worlds which occasionally collide. The first of these is the world of Roman Catholicism in which Catholics around the globe are united by the church's common beliefs and practices. At the center of this world stands the pope who shepherds the entire church on its pilgrim way. United in belief, maintained in prayer, worldwide in scope, and faithful to the past: these are the characteristics of the one, holy, catholic, and apostolic church. The second world is that of American democracy which extols the concepts of majority rule, checks and balances, due process under the law, and inalienable rights. Our sense of fairness is conditioned by these democratic ideals. As citizens in a pluralistic society we respect the right of others to express their views while we reserve the right to disagree with them. Within certain parameters (which are constantly debated) citizens may exercise their right to life, liberty, and the pursuit of happiness.

This chapter focuses on those situations in which the two worlds of Roman Catholics in America come into conflict with each other. For example, in 1968 Pope Paul VI issued the encyclical *Humanae vitae* which forbade the use of artificial contraception. Opinion surveys revealed that large numbers of married Catholic couples did not comply with the teaching. They felt that they could dissent from the church's teaching regarding artificial birth control and remain "good Catholics." Dissent is non-compliance with church teaching. The overarching question under consideration in this chapter is: "Can a member of the Church dissent from church teaching and still be a good Catholic?" We will review the conservative and liberal responses to that question, but first we need to situate this debate in recent church history.

Most historians identify the Second Vatican Council as the most significant event in the life of the church in this century. Two developments which began at Vatican II have a direct impact on the present discussion of dissent in the church. The first is the call for greater collegiality in the church; the second is the definition of the church as the "people of God." Collegiality involves the sharing of authority in the decision making process at all levels in the church, i.e. the pope with the other bishops, the bishops with the priests of the diocese, the pastor with the parishioners. National synods of bishops, priests' senates, and parish councils are rooted in the concept of collegiality. The second development at Vatican II is the emphasis given to the church as the "people of God." This becomes one of the central images of the church in the documents of Vatican II. After Vatican II lay men and women became eucharistic ministers and lectors in their local parishes. The restoration of the permanent deaconate allowed married and single men greater opportunities for ministry in the church.

These two developments undeniably changed the church in highly visible ways, but conservatives and liberals continue to differ over the place of these concepts in the overall understanding of the church. For example, conservatives insist that a recognition of the importance of collegiality does not make the church a democracy. They also argue that the expression "people of God" in no way diminishes the authority of the pope in the church. The church is an institution with clearly defined beliefs and a hierarchial structure of authority. Liberals, on the other hand, charge that the principle of collegiality has not been sufficiently exercised, for instance, in the appointment of bishops. They also charge that the understanding of the church as the people of God leads naturally to the ordination of women and married men to the priesthood.

In the 1980s the issue of dissent once again became a matter of public interest when the Vatican suspended the teaching license of Fr. Charles Curran, a professor of moral theology at The Catholic University of America. Curran was a vocal critic of *Humanae vitae* in 1968 and circulated a statement of opposition to the encyclical in the United States. Curran's liberal views on such volatile subjects as abortion and homosexuality did not go unnoticed by officials at the Vatican. This ongoing dispute between the Vatican and Curran reached its critical point in 1986 when Joseph Cardinal Ratzinger, head of the Congregation for the Doctrine of the Faith, suspended Curran's teaching license. Though focused on the issue of dissent, the Curran affair also raised questions of academic freedom, priestly obedience, and the status of non-infallible teaching. Conservatives and liberals offer radically different assessments of the place of dissent in the church, and, more specifically, of the Vatican's suspension of Curran's teaching license. It is to these differing assessments that we now turn.

Conservative Catholics, insisting that the church must faithfully preserve the truths of the faith, welcomed the suspension of Curran's license. Truth, they argue, is not subject to the changing tides of public opinion. Nor is it determined by majority rule. History is littered with cases of mistaken majorities. Rather, the church has the prophetic responsibility to uphold the truth, even if that truth is rejected by a particular culture. The truth is often unpopular, but it would be ludicrous to suggest that the church should abandon its "tough teachings" and support ones which are more "acceptable."

Conservatives argue further that such dissent endangers

the unity of the church. The church should speak with one voice on matters of faith and morals. Without this loyalty and commitment to church teaching, the church has no unity and its witness in the world is severely handicapped. This type of behavior would not be tolerated in the military or in the corporate world. If employees of a corporation have serious reservations about the company's policy or product, those employees are free to seek employment in a corporation more to their liking. This does not mean that a person must agree with the most minute detail of corporate policy, but a commitment to the "fundamentals" is required. Without a commitment to the central truths of the faith, the church has no real unity. Conservatives argue that a person may disagree with the core of church teaching and still be a moral, loving individual, but not a good Catholic. The church should be a gathering of believers united in one mind and heart. That unity is found in a common commitment to the truths of the faith.

Conservatives also assert the need for the faithful to assent to church teaching as taught by the head of the church, the pope. The pope, they argue, enjoys a unique position in the church. He is the successor to Peter as the head of the church. Our identity as Catholics consists in our acceptance of the pope as the supreme teacher in the church. Curran, in his teaching, was advocating ideas which were clearly in opposition to official church teaching. By suspending his teaching license, Curran's critics maintain, the Vatican was only saying what was plainly clear: Curran's views are not compatible with official church teaching and consequently Curran does not teach authentic Catholic belief. Furthermore, Curran taught at The Catholic University of America, a pontifical university, i.e. one chartered by the Vatican for the purpose of instructing students in Catholic doctrine. Conservatives argue that if Curran wishes to dissent from the teachings of the church, as defined by the pope, he should teach at another university.

Many liberal Catholics who defend Curran contend that the pursuit of truth is the right and obligation of all Catholics. If such a quest is to be carried out with integrity, the church must allow for dissent. An inquiry which at the outset precludes certain conclusions from being drawn is not an open, honest process of reflection. The church must respect the right of Catholics to critique the church's doctrines and, when necessary, to express their reservations or objections. People who disagree with the church are obligated to be well-informed and must allow others the opportunity to raise objections to their positions, but the fundamental openness to truth must be maintained by all members of the church.

Liberals maintain that dissent, despite the unrest and uncertainty which it may provoke, may actually benefit the church. First of all, dissent provokes debate. Such debate forces all parties to rethink their position and formulate counter-arguments. As a result, new theological positions are generated and the intellectual environment is enriched by challenging and lively debate. Second, this atmosphere of charged debate is far superior to a sterile mood of servile acceptance. Liberals charge that the conservative position amounts to making Catholics into robots who blindly accept doctrines which have been handed down to them. A faith which has been questioned, discussed, and finally embraced is preferable to a faith received blindly. Third, dissent may be a sign of vitality, rather than the disunity, of the church. The seriousness of the debate indicates not a disregard for the teachings of the church, but an acknowledgement that such issues are worthy of time and consideration. Intellectual vitality is a sign of a creative, concerned church. If the debate is stifled by fiat from the hierarchy, then this spirit will be dashed. On outward appearances that may amount to a significant decrease in public dissent, but in reality it will simply mean that the willingness to debate these issues has vanished.

Liberals charge the conservatives with offering misleading accounts of the history of church teaching. Liberals contend that the conservatives, by insisting on the need to preserve the truth, overlook the fluidity of church teaching. A number of official and unofficial church practices and teachings have changed over the centuries. Priests were once able to marry. Usury (the practice of charging interest on loans) was once condemned. Civil authorities once selected bishops. Slavery was once accepted as a legitimate social institution. One is not to conclude from this that all teachings and practices of the church are subject to change, but it does serve as a caution against identifying all teachings of the church as equally important. The conservative contention that a body of unchanging truths has been passed down through the centuries in an unbroken chain misrepresents the history of much of church teaching. The call to preserve "the truth" may in fact be a call to return to a practice which did not exist until the nineteenth century.

Liberal Catholics defended Curran's continued presence at Catholic University on the grounds of academic freedom. Catholic universities, even pontifical universities, must allow the free exchange of ideas. To exclude from consideration any position which differs with the official Catholic position violates the very purpose of a university. The Catholic university is the setting where church teaching is scrutinized, where new ideas are presented, and where recommendations for the future are debated. Without this academic freedom to engage in research which might put church teaching in a new light or offer speculation on how church teaching might change, the integrity of Catholic universities is jeopardized. To put prior constraints on what conclusions may be drawn from a discussion undercuts the credibility of the Catholic universities as genuine institutions of higher learning. They will become nothing more than catechism classes where the students learn statements of belief by rote. Furthermore, Curran's dissent concerned non-infallible teaching. He was challenging those teachings which have not been declared infallibly true by the pope. Questioning of such teaching, contend the liberals, must be acceptable, especially in a university setting.

Does dissent tear apart the unity of the church or is it a necessity which actually promotes a healthy environment within the church? Clearly wisdom is needed here. Not all beliefs are of equal importance. Picture in your mind a bull's-eye target. The center of the target is surrounded by concentric circles. The center of the target would contain the fundamental beliefs of Roman Catholicism. For example, Catholicism has an obvious stake in the claim that Jesus existed. If Jesus never existed, but was a fictional character invented by a group of authors in the first century, then Christianity would be in trouble. On the farthest ring of the target would be beliefs which are incidental to Christianity. If a person disagrees with the recommendations for the length of the wax candles, this is not to be taken as an assault on the core of the Christian faith.

This idea that there is a core set of beliefs is accepted by both liberals and conservatives. In their *Decree on Ecumenism*, the bishops at Vatican II asserted that "in Catholic teaching there exists an order or 'hierarchy' of truths, since they vary in their relationship to the foundation of the Christian faith" (n. 11). This provides a helpful way of dealing with the question of dissent, but it clearly leaves a major question unresolved. The problem arises when one must locate the various beliefs on the rings of the target. For example, is belief in papal infallibility at the core of the faith or is it peripheral? Some Catholics may consider the centralization of papal authority as a development of the modern age whereas others see it as integral to Roman

Catholicism from its earliest days. Where on the target should we place adherence to *Humanae vitae?* Where is weekly mass attendance? When have we crossed the line and lost the faith? When must the church maintain its standards? When should the church show compassion? If the standards are maintained, are certain groups unnecessarily excluded from the life of the church? If compassion is shown, do the laws of the church count for nothing? These questions confront every parish in the country. Is it permissible to set aside certain masses for divorced Catholics? Is it acceptable to allow groups of gay Catholics who wish to discuss their concerns in the context of the Catholic faith to publicize their meetings in the church bulletin? Should a priest in any way criticize the pope during a homily or public address? The dilemma of dissent affects all levels of church government, from the local churches to the universal church.

The dilemma of dissent requires that we balance two legitimate concerns. On the one hand, the church must safeguard its beliefs. It has the right to declare certain views as incompatible with Roman Catholicism. In theological terminology, the church has the right and duty to identify "heresy." On the other hand, church teaching must be subject to close scrutiny. Respectful dialogue does no harm to the church. Disagreement must not be mistaken for disloyalty. Within those parameters, however, a good deal of heated debate is likely to take place among American Roman Catholics for some time to come.

DISCUSSION QUESTIONS

1. Is dissent a good thing or a bad thing for the church? State your reasons. Anticipate objections and respond to them.

2. Evaluate the arguments put forth by both liberals and conservatives. What are the strengths and weaknesses of each position?

3. What degree of dissent is tolerable?

4. How would you have handled the Curran case?

SUGGESTED READING

The April 25, 1987 issue of *America* contains an article by Curran and various other articles representing a spectrum of opinion on Curran's case.

For a book length defense by Curran and a chronology of the events surrounding his case, see Charles Curran, *Faithful Dissent* (Kansas City: Sheed & Ward, 1986).

For a more detailed discussion of the issues, see Philip S. Kaufman, O.S.B., *Why You Can Disagree . . . And Remain a Faithful Catholic* (Bloomington: Meyers-Stone, 1989).

The cover story of the September 7, 1987 issue of *Time* deals with the state of American Catholicism.

For a scholarly discussion of the issues, see William W. May, ed., *Vatican Authority and American Catholic Dissent: The Curran Case and Its Consequences* (New York: Crossroad, 1987).

The Dilemma of the Christian Community and the World

Is the world our enemy or our friend?

A theological dilemma arises from the very fact that Christians find themselves living out their lives in the midst of a given culture with its distinctive social, political, and economic institutions. These elements comprise "the world" in which the church must exist. There is by necessity a relationship between the church and the world, but what should that relationship be? In the Christian tradition, two general responses can be discerned. The first is an outward embrace of the wider culture with a desire to present the Christian faith in a way which is meaningful and relevant to Christians and non-Christians alike. The second is an inward concentration on the Christian community with a desire to embody the Christian faith to the fullest extent so that the church can serve as a counter-cultural witness to the world.

Both stances toward the world ground themselves in the Christian scriptures. Those favoring the outward movement of the church toward the world call attention to the numerous missionary passages in the scriptures. Throughout Jesus' ministry we find him teaching, healing, and performing various miracles in the villages and cities and commanding the apostles to do the same, e.g. "So (the Twelve) set out and went from village to village, spreading the good news everywhere and curing diseases" (Lk 9:6). At the close of Matthew's gospel Jesus, after being raised from the dead, commands the apostles to "make disciples of all the nations." The entire book of Acts chronicles the spread of the Christian movement from Jerusalem to Rome. In addition to this strong missionary (or "outward") impulse, the Christian scriptures repeatedly highlight the radical call of Jesus. "He summoned the crowd with his disciples and said to them: 'If a man wishes to come after me, he must deny his very self, take up his cross, and follow in my steps' " (Mk 8:34). Those favoring an inward concentration on the life of the church argue that this radically new way of life often puts Christians at odds with the world. John's gospel captures this experience well. In his farewell discourse, Jesus leaves his disciples with this thought: "If you find that the world hates you, know it has hated me before you. If you belonged to the world, it would love you as its own; the reason it hates you is that you do not belong to the world" (15:18–19).

Proponents of each position wish to preserve what they consider to be an essential dimension of Christianity. Those favoring an outward movement into the world feel that the Christian life consists of spreading the gospel through all available means so that the gospel can be meaningful and relevant to the lives of individual Christians as well as beneficial to the wider society. Those advocating an inward concentration argue that the Christian life consists in forming communities of believers to serve as powerful witnesses to the truth of the gospel. In theological literature, a distinction is often drawn between a church and a sect. This terminology may be confusing since both terms refer to the Christian community or "the church." Nevertheless, Christians who feel that the Christian community should act as a "church" favor the outward movement into the world. Those Christians who favor the inward concentration see the Christian community as a "sect."

The outward movement associated with the "church" type sees the Christian community as involved in a partnership with the world. In terms of the church's relationship with the political order, this partnership can take two forms. In the first, the church and state have identical goals. In the second the church and state have separate, though complementary goals. In the first case, the church gives its blessing to the political leader (e.g., the king), perhaps regarding the ruler as God's representative on earth. This ensures the loyalty of the church members to the throne. In return, the authority of the church is backed by the might of the king. The law of the land will protect the church and support its teachings. The church enjoys the protection of the military and may receive financial assistance from the state. In some cases, heretics may be tried in civil courts and, if found guilty, punished by the state. In the second arrangement, the state and the church both play a necessary role in the life of a nation. Roughly speaking, the state provides the support for the material needs of the people and the church attends to the spiritual needs of the people. The state would not directly interfere in church affairs and the church would abide by similar limitations on its power, but the two realms would be closely linked. The political power of the church would be indirect, though effective.

The inward or sectarian approach sees the Christian community and the world in opposition to one another. Sectarians withdraw from the world for a variety of reasons, e.g. to create an environment which is more conducive to spiritual development, to avoid the ills of the wider society or to provide the world with a powerful witness to holiness. For whatever reason the separation takes place, the resulting relationship between the Christian community and the world ranges from hostility to a detached concern. Active persecution by the state creates the greatest strain between the two parties. During this persecution the state is seen as the very embodiment of evil as it goes about killing the holy ones of God. Conflict may arise between the accepted morality of the culture and that of the Christian community. Like passengers fleeing a sinking ship, these sectarians see separation from the world as necessary for their spiritual survival. Other sectarians may leave the world in order to pursue singlemindedly the life of prayer. They may not regard the world as overly corrupt, but simply as filled with distractions. Finally, some sectarians may feel that the best way to improve the world is to stand apart from it and create a different model for human relations which is better than the one presently at work in the society.

Two different responses to the question of relationship between Christians and the "authorities" can be found in the Christian scriptures. A scene taken from the book of Acts demonstrates well the defiant stance Christians have taken toward the authorities. The Jewish authorities are displeased with the apostles and order them to stop preaching about Jesus. When the high priest complains that the apostles have disobeyed their orders, Peter simply says, "Better for us to obey God than men" (6:29). Despite the urgings of a certain Pharisee named Gamaliel to leave the Christians alone, the Jewish judicial body known as the Sanhedrin orders that the apostles be whipped and again ordered not to preach about Jesus. The apostles continue to preach in direct defiance of the Sanhedrin's orders. The contrasting scriptural passage is Romans 13. Here Paul discusses the proper relationship between Christians and the civil authorities. "Let everyone obey the authorities that are over him, for there is no authority except from God, and all authority that exists is established by God. As a consequence, the man who opposes authority rebels against the ordinance of God; those who resist thus shall draw condemnation down upon themselves" (13:1–2). The ruler is "God's servant" who carries out the decrees of God. To resist the ruler is to resist God since God has placed authority in the hands of the ruler. No clearer scriptural statement can be found in support of a strong church-state alliance.

Proponents of the "church" view of the Christian community argue that the outward movement toward the world offers a number of advantages. First of all, the involvement in the world enables the church to be an effective agent for social change. The church may bring about this change either directly or indirectly. The church may encourage the state to provide housing for the homeless, education for the poor, or health care for the elderly. The church could also provide direct relief for the disadvantaged (e.g. shelters, soup kitchens). The church could also act indirectly in the process of social change by instilling Christian values in the culture. As a result, the society as a whole sees the importance of providing assistance to the needy or treating all persons equally under the law. By withdrawing from the world, the sectarians leave the political process to be run by others who may or may not share their values. Second, the outward church movement sees the world as inherently good. Despite the sin which undeniably exists in the world, the fundamental goodness of creation and humanity endures. Christians can look upon non-Christians as people of good will and see the world around as filled with opportunities for cooperative efforts aimed at creating a more just society. As the bishops at Vatican II concluded, "Hence it is clear that men are not deterred by the Christian message from building up the world, or impelled to neglect the welfare of their fellows. They are, rather, more stringently bound to do these very things."

Critics charge that the church approach is not without its dangers. The most pernicious danger is the confusion of political or cultural aspirations with the mandates of the gospel. This is most clearly evident with strong church-state alliances. The tighter the relationship between the church and the state the more likely the fate of one is linked with the fate of the other. This is most evident at times of war, though this is certainly not the only instance. Suppose a nation's policy of colonialism provides generous economic benefits to the nation and a large number of converts to the church. Is there a temptation not to question the appropriateness of such policies or the methods by which these economic gains have been acquired and these converts have been won over to the faith? Churches too often resist challenging an injustice which has popular support for fear that such a challenge will alienate the church from the state and thus diminish the church's ability to influence public policy in the future. Sectarians see such compromise with the state as a betrayal of the radical call of Jesus. Did the churches in the United States call for an immediate end to slavery? Did the German churches deplore the anti-semitism of the Nazis? If they did not, the sectarians argue, then they failed to be signs of God's light in a world shrouded in darkness.

By concentrating on the inner life of the church, the sectarians feel that they are better able to take prophetic stands. They insist that they preserve their critical edge by standing apart from the concerns of the state or the wider society. With their attention focused on the Christian perspective, the sectarians claim to be less willing to engage in political compromise. They prefer to stand apart from the political process and evaluate the activities of the state from their own Christian perspective. In addition to this, the sectarian remains critical of the attitudes and values of the wider culture. For instance, a society may subtly, or not so subtly, endorse the idea that a person's worth is directly proportional to a person's wealth. This attitude may find expression and reinforcement in advertising and television shows. The sectarian seems more willing and better able to identify these types of messages and denounce them in the name of the gospel.

Those in the church perspective contend that the purity which the sectarians seek so tenaciously carries some costs as well. The most troublesome would be their lack of involvement in the life of the society. They seem less willing to work in the midst of ambiguity. Questions of a political nature seem to defy easy and quick solutions. In part this is because of the political process itself, but it is also the case that some questions simply do not have easy answers. Honorable men and women may disagree on how to balance the budget or how to reform the educational system. Politics also requires a willingness to accept a solution which enjoys widespread support, though it may in fact fall short of one's own expectations. The sectarians, by preferring to stand apart from that process, preserve their integrity, but at the expense of not providing input into a system which could benefit those in need. Second, critics charge that the sectarians run the danger of seeing "the world" as corrupt or unworthy of the attention of Christians. This outlook runs the very serious danger of allowing injustice to continue unchecked. Third, the sectarians isolate the church from new trends of thought in the hope that such trends will not find their way into the Christian community and alter the beliefs and practices of Christians. However, new thought is not necessarily a threat to Christianity. Even if the thought conflicts with Christian belief, engagement of that nature might actually benefit the church by forcing it to creatively use its intellectual energies to counter the rival claims.

The debate between the church and sect advocates is often framed as a battle between the realists and the idealists. The debate revolves around the word "compromise." The realists see compromise in a positive light; it is a necessary feature of life, but most especially political life. In their view, compromise between church and state allows for small, but real gains in developing a more just society. The benefits, in other words, outweigh the costs. The sectarians view compromise in a negative light. Too much self-interest can be justified in the name of compromise. The church must be faithful to its call at whatever cost. To do less than that is an act of cowardice. The story of the life and death of Luis Espinal, S.J. provides a powerful testimony to this belief. Fr. Espinal was a gifted filmmaker and journalist who turned his talents in the last twelve years of his life to documenting the life of the poor in Bolivia. Ignoring the death threats, Espinal continued to denounce the brutality of the military which ruled the country. As a result, he was kidnaped, tortured for four hours, and finally killed. On the spot where a poor Indian peasant found his body someone has placed a marker which reads, "[Jesus Christ] give us the sincerity not to call cowardice conformity and convenience prudence." Many would argue that Fr. Espinal foolishly acted in a way which would almost certainly bring about his death and deprive the poor of a valued ally. Others would insist that Fr. Espinal's foolishness consisted of nothing less than living out the gospel message with wholehearted dedication.

Others speak of this debate as a choice between quantity and quality. The outward approach is more willing to gather into the fold members of various degrees of commitment. The hope, of course, is that through time the church can raise their level of understanding and commitment. The sectarians, on the other hand, tend to gather together persons who already have a deep commitment to the cause. The hope in this case is that such a gathering will provide a powerful witness to the world.

The stance of the church toward the world depends on a number of factors which change over time, e.g. the degree to which Christians using the political process have successfully brought about change and the extent to which the values of the culture cohere with Christian values. Different situations call for different strategies. The Catholic experience in America provides an interesting case study. In the second half of the last century, immigrant Catholics arrived in large numbers on the shores of the United States. These immigrants wished to show that their Catholicism did not in any way interfere with their patriotism. Slowly Catholics gained acceptance into American society. The election of John F. Kennedy demonstrated the success with which Catholic Americans had forged a bond between their religious faith and their democratic ideals. This alliance between Catholic loyalty and American patriotism would be tested in the 1960s and 1970s. Three major events generated some reassessment on the part of American Catholics. The Vietnam War and the Watergate scandal brought about a different cultural mood in the country. There was a greater skepticism toward the government, and though this sentiment was certainly not confined to Catholics, the seeds were sown for a different attitude among American Catholics toward the government. The third event proved decisive. The 1973 Supreme Court decision in the case of Roe v. Wade held that a woman's constitutional right to privacy guaranteed her the right to have an abortion during the first six months of pregnancy. This pitted official Catholic teaching regarding abortion against the finding of the highest court of the land. Since the Roe v. Wade decision, the American bishops have become more willing to express public criticism of the government. For example, in their 1983 pastoral letter "The Challenge of Peace: God's Promise and Our Response" the bishops raised objections to American military strategy. The bishops condemned the "first use" of nuclear weapons: "We do not perceive any situation in which the deliberate initiation of nuclear warfare, on however restricted a scale, can be morally justified." The future course of American Catholicism is difficult to chart, but both inward and outward impulses can be discerned at the present time. Most pro-life advocates have chosen the course of political involvement in order to achieve their goals. Other smaller groups have chosen the route of prophetic witness and civil disobedience to protest U.S. policies toward Central America or the arms race.

What does it mean to be a disciple of Christ in today's world? Certainly there is no more important question upon which Christians should reflect. This question asks us to endorse one of two positions concerning discipleship. Do Christians more faithfully follow Jesus by moving out toward the world with the risk that they may compromise the gospel, or by withdrawing from the world with the risk of rending the gospel irrelevant to the life of the wider society? The choice between church and sect, be it a debate between realism and idealism or quantity and quality, is at its core a question of how to be a member of the Christian community in today's world.

DISCUSSION QUESTIONS

1. To what extent does the American society embody Christian values?
2. Do you view the Christian community primarily as a church or a sect?
3. When, if ever, should a Christian disobey a civil law?
4. Is compromise a good thing or a bad thing?

SUGGESTED READINGS

A fine summary of the different options Christians have pursued in terms of relating to the world can be found in Chapters Eight and Nine of Mary Jo Weaver's *Introduction to Christianity* (Belmont: Wadsworth Publishing Co., 1984).

H. Richard Niebuhr's *Christ and Culture* (New York: Harper & Row, 1951) continues to play a significant role in the discussion.

For a short introduction to the history of Roman Catholic social thought, see the introduction to *Renewing the Earth: Catholic Documents on Peace, Justice, and Liberation* (Garden City: Doubleday, 1977), edited by David J. O'Brien and Thomas A. Shannon, pp. 11–43.

Advanced theological students may wish to read Ernst Troeltsch's *The Social Teaching of the Christian Churches* (Chicago: University of Chicago Press, 1981, originally London: George Allen & Unwin Ltd., 1931) pp. 331–43, John Howard Yoder's *The Christian Witness to the State* (Newton: Faith and Life Press, 1964), and Charles Curran's *American Catholic Social Ethics: Twentieth-Century Approaches* (Notre Dame: University of Notre Dame Press, 1982) for overviews of the different approaches to relating the gospel to the culture.

See also Richard P. McBrien's *Caesar's Coin: Religion and Politics in America* (New York: Macmillan, 1987). For a collection of essays from the sectarian perspective, see Stanley Hauerwas *A Community of Character* (Notre Dame: University of Notre Dame Press, 1981), especially Chapter Five.

For a collection of essays from the church perspective, see *The Church and Culture Since Vatican II: The Experience of North and Latin America,* edited by Joseph Gremillion (Notre Dame: University of Notre Dame Press, 1985).

The Dilemma of Christian Ethics

*How do we decide what's right
and what's wrong?*

How should we live our lives? The simplicity of the question masks its profundity. Even with the greatest sincerity to do the right thing, a person may be uncertain about what choice to make when confronting difficult moral questions. Should we remove long term comatose patients from life support systems? Should we allow genetic engineering? Should minorities be given preferential treatment in college admissions? The sense of uncertainty arises not from the person's lack of ethical conviction, but from the complexity of the questions themselves. This chapter does not attempt to resolve specific moral issues, but rather focuses on how people go about making ethical decisions. Two dilemmas will be explored: "Is there a universal ethic which is binding on all people?" and "Is there any rule which may never be violated or any action which may never be performed?" A discussion of this type serves the useful purpose of exposing some of the presuppositions which are operative in our ethical reasoning. By subjecting these presuppositions to close scrutiny, we are able to refine our reasoning process and in doing so enable ourselves to examine specific ethical issues more completely.

We begin with the question, "Is there a universal ethic which is binding on all people?" In order to answer this question, let us suppose that radical terrorists highjack an airliner bound for New York City to protest U.S. foreign policy toward their country. In order to demonstrate their seriousness, the terrorists kill one of the American passengers. The terrorists' supporters hail the highjacking as a courageous act of protest and regard the killing of the American as just retribution for policies of the United States government. The U.S. public is outraged by the highjacking which it calls an unjust act of aggression toward innocent persons and denounces the killing of the American as a cowardly and evil act.

The scenario leaves unanswered the question: Who is right? Was the taking of the airliner an ethical thing to do? Was the killing of the passenger morally justified? One group of ethicists would insist there is an "objective moral order" or universal ethic. An "objective" moral order exists independently of the individual's perceptions or opinions of what is right and wrong. For example, the taking of innocent human life is morally wrong. Even if in the mind of a killer it is justified or if it has become an accepted practice of a particular culture, it is nonetheless wrong. No matter what people perceive to be the morally correct position, there is a moral truth. If they hold a position contrary to the moral truth, they are in error. A second group of thinkers would argue that judgments about right and wrong are "relative." In this view, what is right in one culture may be wrong in another. There is no universal ethic binding on all people. For example, western society looks upon cannibalism as a morally repugnant act, but in certain tribal cultures it is an accepted practice. In fact, the consumption of the elder's brain is perceived as the means by which the elder's wisdom is passed to the next generation. The airliner incident represents a similar clash of moralities. What is praised in one culture is condemned in another.

The objectivists and relativists offer different accounts of how people come to an understanding of right and wrong. The objectivists claim that through human reason we are able to discern certain moral truths. We are able to do this because there is a structure to reality and our mind can understand this structure. This structure or "natural law" determines the proper course of action. Behavior which complies with the natural law is moral; that which violates this natural law is immoral. For example, there is a natural inclination toward self-preservation. This instinct or drive is built into the very being of humans. Suicide violates the natural drive toward self-preservation and consequently must be seen as immoral. The relativists locate the origin of concepts of right and wrong in the culture. One's upbringing determines a person's sense of appropriate and inappropriate behavior. Radically different cultures often differ sharply over what constitutes proper behavior. All actions must be judged by the standard of the culture in which it was performed. What is proper behavior in one place at one time might very well be improper at another place at another time.

This "objective" or "natural law" approach to ethics has a number of appealing features. First of all, its universality provides the basis for international discussion about human rights and justice. By virtue of their common humanity, persons of radically different backgrounds can enter into profitable dialogue about ethical matters. Second, the moral life is seen as a fulfillment of our basic nature. The natural law is not imposed upon us as some alien force; it is who we are. Finally, the existence of objective moral truths allows for criticism of civil law. If there is no law other than we humans devise, then there can be no appeal to a "higher law." The leaders of the civil rights movement disobeyed the segregation laws of various states because they were deemed unjust. The equality and dignity of all humans, regardless of color, was seen as a higher law than the law of a particular state.

The "objective" approach is not without its problems. The chief difficulty is determining what is "natural." For example, are humans peaceful or aggressive by nature? The resolution of that question has tremendous implications for how we evaluate acts of violence and participation in warfare. There appears to be ample evidence to support both claims. Is "natural" to be determined by reason or by observing the behavior of animals in the wild? Few ethicists would argue that life in the wild should serve as the standard for human behavior. How do we differentiate the natural law from a long-standing custom? For example, is monogamy natural? Is monogamous marriage an institution created for social convenience or is it rooted in the very nature of humans? It is very difficult to determine the answer to these and other questions, yet questions such as these strike at the heart of the claim that there exists an "objective" standard for all persons.

The second difficulty confronting the objective approach is of a theological nature. If we are sufficiently guided by our reason in matters of ethical significance, what role does Christ play? Do his teachings repeat the natural law? contradict the natural law? go beyond the natural law? If they repeat the natural law, then they are redundant. If they contradict the natural law, then they violate the structure which God put in place. If they go beyond the natural law, then Christians must live according to different standards than other people. But how do we disentangle the natural law commands from those which are "beyond" the natural law (and therefore applicable only to Christians)?

The relativist perspective includes a number of different positions. The most extreme position would deny the existence of any universal moral truths and insist that all values are culturally dependent. Those who argue this position find themselves in the paradoxical bind of saying that all truths are relative, but that relativism itself is universal. Others will allow some universal inclination to do the good, but would argue that "the good" or "justice" is determined by the particular culture. Other relativists make the more modest claim that the discussion of universal truths proves ultimately unsatisfying and in its place we should begin with the recognition that all thought is conditioned by the culture. Different groups should then identify common values and establish a shared framework for ethical discussion. This last position will be the model of relativism discussed below.

This "softer" form of relativism seems to render an accurate account of how the world actually is. Through historical study we have gained a greater understanding of the customs of ancient cultures. Through mass media we have been exposed to the various cultures within our world at the present time. The relativist recognizes the tremendous formative power of culture on all thought, especially ethics. The relativist can acknowledge a high degree of cultural diversity without feeling compelled to make immediate moral judgements about those differences. The relativist does not assume there is some universal standpoint from which all positions must be measured; therefore, the relativist approaches ethical dialogue differently than would an objectivist. If there is only one correct position (which typically happens to be the position espoused by the objectivist), then the other party is simply in error. The danger is imperialism. Armed with the truth, the objectivist might "correct" the "backward" or "unenlightened" habits of the other party. The treatment of both native Americans by the settlers of this country and native inhabitants of other countries by Christian missionaries often testifies to the inherent dangers of this type of thinking. The relativist is less prone to such imperialism since the position does not justify such an approach.

The most troublesome danger of relativism appears at times of moral outrage. Is the expression of moral outrage simply the venting of emotions arising out of a violation of a particular culture's values or is it something more universal? The horrors of the holocaust and other atrocities provoke deeply felt reactions of disgust. But the danger of relativism is that this disgust could amount to nothing more than one group saying to another, "We think what you did was wrong." If the other group should respond, "We think what we did was fine," the ethical debate has quickly reached a permanent impasse. Are we unable to condemn in any meaningful way the torture of political prisoners in foreign countries or acts of terrorism perpetrated against innocent victims? If both parties in the ethical dialogue share a sufficient number of ethical commitments, then a profitable exchange of views can ensue. Without that common ground, it seems moral criticism amounts to nothing more than a statement of opinion.

These two approaches, with their respective strengths and weaknesses, lead to different types of moral reasoning and argumentation. In the objectivist approach the person tends to rely upon reason, common sense, or perhaps intuition. The arguments are framed in such a way that will be acceptable in "public" discourse. "Public" language makes no appeal to any sources beyond what is accepted by all participants in the discussion. For example, in American political discussion appeals to the Constitution are fitting and proper. By contrast, the relativist approach offers reasons framed in language which is not universally shared (i.e. public) such as religious language. Appeals to scripture may prove persuasive in the church, but not in the public forum. The objectivist sees such appeals as ineffective or inappropriate since the position can just as easily be presented in public language. The discussion of the Christian community as church or sect ties in here. The church type would be inclined toward public discourse while the sectarian would prefer the more particularistic type of argumentation.

The second question for consideration is: Is there any rule which may never be violated or any action which may never be performed regardless of the consequences? This question asks whether there are any rules which are so fundamental to the moral life that their violation would consistently cause an unambiguously immoral act to result? Are there any actions which are inherently evil and must never be performed no matter what benefits the actions may bring? This type of question asks us to examine the extent to which we look to consequences to determine the rightness or wrongness of an action.

There is general feeling that there are exceptions to every rule, so let us begin by scrutinizing this idea. A group of thinkers known as utilitarians are most often associated with this position. The leading thinkers of this tradition are John Stuart Mill and Jeremy Bentham. The utilitarians derive their name from the concept of "utility" which has to do with how useful an action or rule is in bringing about the best state of affairs. The utilitarians consider the ethical thing to be that which gives "the greatest good for the greatest number." The goal is to maximize the benefits and minimize the drawbacks. The consequences which follow from a rule or action, therefore, play a significant part in the evaluation of that rule or action. An action or rule which produces a number of benefits with minimal drawbacks is deemed ethically superior to a rule or action which produces numerous drawbacks and minimal benefits.

In opposition to the utilitarians there are those who insist that certain rules are exception-less or that certain actions are always immoral. An ethic which does not allow for exceptions is said to be "deontological," coming from the word for "duty" (*deon*). Certain commandments from God may be seen as deontological (e.g. the ten commandments). The foremost philosophical advocate of this approach is Immanuel Kant. Kant, for example, argued that we should always treat persons as ends in themselves and never as means to an end. Kant also felt that we should act on any maxim whereby we can at the same time will that it should be a universal law. For example, since we could not will that lying should be universal law, we cannot lie. Even if there is a situation when a lie would prove beneficial to a large number of people, lying is always wrong.

As Kant would say, "Let justice be done though the heavens fall." One's duty must be done, regardless of consequences.

An example might clarify the differences between the utilitarian and deontological approaches. Suppose a man is murdered in a very small town. Suppose further that the sheriff of that town rounds up ten men whom he feels are likely suspects, though he has no evidence to support his charge. In fact, all ten men are innocent of the crime. He and his deputies handcuff the ten men and lead them out into a deserted field where he fastens the string of handcuffed men to two trees. The sheriff stands before the ten men and informs them of his suspicion that the murderer stands before him and of his intention to "solve" this crime before the night is through. When no one confesses to the murder, the sheriff turns to the first man and says, "I saw you around the time of the crime, so you must be innocent. But I'm certain that one of the remaining nine is guilty. Tell me who killed the man or I will kill them all one by one." Suppose as well that the taking of the lives of these nine men could be easily concealed and no agencies would investigate their disappearance. What should the man do? The utilitarian would probably argue that the man should randomly select one man and identify him as the murderer. In this way, one man dies while nine live. The deontological approach would say that it is always wrong to kill the innocent. No matter what consequences may follow, the proper choice would be to refrain from condemning an innocent person to death.

Utilitarianism has a number of attractive features as an ethical system; of them three are particularly noteworthy. First of all, utilitarianism's greatest strength is its practicality. The utilitarian ideal of maximizing the benefits while minimizing the losses strikes as an appropriate way of dealing with a "no win" situation. In this way, utilitarianism looks at the ethical life with a common sense wisdom. There will be tragic situations in which the choice will not be between good and evil, but rather between the lesser of two evils. Utilitarianism is well equipped for such situations. Second, utilitarianism places great emphasis on consequences. Again this strikes us as commonsensical, but the effects of one's actions should, it seems reasonable to suggest, factor into our ethical deliberation. Implied in this is a sense of responsibility for one's actions, a willingness to be held accountable for the effect one's choice has on others. Finally, utilitarianism gives great latitude for the expression of personal liberty. The pursuit of one's desires, be they financial, artistic, or political, is restricted only by considerations of fairness for the whole of society. These restrictions protect the personal liberties of others so that liberty and justice are maximized in the society.

Despite the considerable advantages of utilitarianism, utilitarians must face some troublesome questions. First of all, can we fully anticipate all the consequences of our actions? Utilitarianism operates on the underlying assumption that we can determine all consequences of action A and all consequences of action B and determine on the basis of that information "the greatest good for the greatest number." For example, we have become increasingly aware of the unanticipated effects past actions have had on the present environmental conditions, e.g. industrial emissions in one country cause acid rain in other countries, the reduction of tropical rain forests causes global warming, and the illegal disposal of hazardous waste contaminates ground water for neighboring communities. Second, once an exception of any kind is allowed, what prevents further exceptions? This objection is commonly referred to as a "slippery slope" argument. It resembles the climber on a slippery slope who drops to the bottom because nothing prevents the fall. Without a solid, definitive prohibition, exceptions will follow one after the other. Each exception is a step down "the slippery slope." Third, on questions of social policy, who determines the "greatest good for the greatest number"? Do we put it to a vote? Do we allow the elected officials to make those determinations? Do we turn to the Supreme Court, or is it the duty of the president to make such decisions?

The deontological ethicists look upon utilitarianism as a distortion and perversion of the ethical life. Utilitarian reasoning could justify any number of actions which the deontological thinker would deem immoral. Might it not be in the best interest of the whole to eliminate certain members of the community who are "burdensome"? Would such a nightmarish suggestion be acceptable on utilitarian grounds? It is, at the very least, theoretically possible. Utilitarians will constantly have to deal with the problem of the "slippery slope." Any prohibitions which are put in place to secure the greatest good for the greatest number of people are subject to revision or elimination. By disregarding consequences, the deontological thinkers feel they have preserved the integrity of the ethical life. When duty is done simply for duty's sake, then justice is truly "blind." The action is not tainted by self-interest or the fear of attack or ostracism. With exception-less prohibitions in place, clear boundaries are set between acceptable and unacceptable actions, or, simply put, between right and wrong.

The utilitarians charge that the deontological approach is in fact the distorted view of the ethical life. Its rigidity makes it unacceptable as an ethical theory. The utilitarians charge that it is possible, for example, to imagine a situation in which lying is "the ethical thing to do." Suppose a woman invites a neighbor over for lunch. While eating lunch, another neighbor who suffers from mental illness and has a history of violent behavior comes to the door and angrily asks for the whereabouts of her lunch guest who he claims is plotting to kill him. Should the woman tell the man at the door that the neighbor he seeks is sitting in the kitchen? Common sense and prudence teach us that it would be a wise decision to deny any knowledge of the neighbor's whereabouts. The deontological thinkers who advocate exception-less prohibitions fail to take into account the situation in which decisions must be made. There are legitimate reasons for overriding even the most basic of ethical principles, such as truth-telling. The utilitarians insist that the burden of proof lies with the person who tells the lie, but hold that it is possible that sufficient reasons could be given for the violation of even the most cherished rules of ethics.

The ethical life is a process of discerning right from wrong. The Christian ethical life, more specifically, is a discernment of what it means to be a disciple of Jesus Christ. A discussion of the two dilemmas presented here, it is hoped, will bring some small measure of clarity and insight to both pursuits.

Discussion Questions

1. Is there an objective moral order? Defend your position against possible objections.
2. Are there any actions which are universally condemned?
3. Which is a more persuasive reason not to do something—because it is "unnatural" or because it is "un-Christian"?
4. Assume the dropping of the bomb on Hiroshima (a) killed innocent Japanese citizens and (b) ended the war earlier. Was it a moral or immoral action?
5. Are there any actions which are "intrinsically evil"? In other words, are there any actions which can never be justified for any reason whatsoever?

SUGGESTED READING

Fagothey's Right and Reason, revised by Milton A. Gonsalves (Columbus: Charles E. Merrill Publishing Co., 1986) provides a helpful introduction to relativism, natural law theory, utilitarianism, and Kantian ethics.

A slightly more difficult text, but one which summarizes well the major positions on the questions discussed here, is *What Are They Saying About Moral Norms?* (Ramsey: Paulist, 1982) by Richard M. Gula, S.S.

Advanced theological students would benefit from reading James M. Gustafson's *Protestant and Roman Catholic Ethics: Prospects for Rapprochement* (Chicago: University of Chicago Press, 1978) for an overview of the different approaches in Christian ethics.

For a defense of the natural law approach to Christian ethics, see Timothy E. O'Connell's *Principles for a Catholic Morality* (New York: Seabury, 1978).

For a defense of a particularistic approach to Christian ethics, see Stanley Hauerwas' *The Peaceable Kingdom: A Primer in Christian Ethics* (Notre Dame: University of Notre Dame Press, 1983).

The Dilemma of Christian Commitment

Do promises always mean forever?

Christians often speak of being "called by God" or "having a vocation" when citing reasons for making certain pivotal choices in their lives. In the Roman Catholic tradition this calling may be realized in the single, married, or religious life. When entering into these states of life people typically vow to remain faithful to their chosen way of life until death. The reality is, however, that for a variety of reasons couples divorce, priests are laicized, and sisters and brothers leave their orders. How should the Christian community look upon this situation? Some Christians argue that these vowed commitments are sacred and as such may not be broken; others contend that in certain cases persons may be released from such vows. In the first half of this chapter we will examine the Roman Catholic Church's understanding of marriage and its position on divorce; in the second half we will move to a general examination of the nature of commitment and the possibility of release from vowed commitment.

The official teaching of the Roman Catholic Church is that "A valid marriage between baptized persons that has been consummated cannot be dissolved by any human power or by any cause except by death." A fuller elaboration of this teaching of the church requires exploration of two somewhat complicated topics. The first concerns the concept of "validity" and the practice of granting annulments. The second concerns the scriptural writings dealing with divorce.

The concept of "validity" plays a major role in the church's understanding of marriage. The term validity means, according to James Hardon, "that certain prescriptions must be fulfilled for the law or contractual agreement to bind or take effect." One of the prescriptions concerning marriage is age. Canon law (i.e. the laws governing the church) states that "A man cannot validly enter marriage before the completion of his sixteenth year of age, nor a woman before the completion of her fourteenth year" (Canon 1083). Another requirement would be that the two parties freely enter into the marriage. "A marriage is invalid which was entered into by reason of force or of grave fear imposed from outside, even if not purposely, from which the person has no escape other than by choosing marriage" (Canon 1103). Marriages which do not meet requirements such as these are said to be invalid, and invalid marriages are non-binding.

The concept of validity underlies the Roman Catholic Church's practice of granting annulments. The church does not recognize divorces of validly married Catholics; however, the church does grant annulments. An annulment decrees that, in the eyes of the church, no true marriage ever existed. The determination whether or not to grant an annulment is usually made by the marriage tribunal of a diocese. It is important to note that any children born to the couple are not considered illegitimate.

The second source of complication in this discussion is the lack of uniformity in the scriptural teaching on divorce. In Mark's gospel, we read:

Then some Pharisees came up and as a test began to ask him whether it was permissible for a husband to divorce his wife. In reply he said, "What command did Moses give you?" They answered, "Moses permitted divorce and the writing of the decree of divorce." But Jesus told them: "He wrote that commandment for you because of your stubbornness. At the beginning of creation God made them male and female; for this reason a man shall leave his father and mother and the two shall become as one. They are no longer two but one flesh. Therefore let no man separate what God has joined." Back in the house again, the disciples began to question him about this. He told them, "Whoever divorces his wife and marries another commits adultery against her; and the woman who divorces her husband and marries another commits adultery" (10:2–12).

This passage presents a fairly straightforward condemnation of divorce by Jesus. In Matthew's gospel, written after Mark's gospel, we do not find this absolute prohibition against divorce. Matthew records Jesus' teaching on divorce as follows: "What I say to you is: everyone who divorces his wife—lewd conduct is a separate case—forces her to commit adultery. The man who marries a divorced woman likewise commits adultery" (5:32). We need not concern ourselves with the debate over the proper interpretation of the Greek word (i.e. *porneia*, translated here as "lewd conduct") which Matthew uses to identify the exceptional case. Some argue that the term refers to sexual infidelity while other scholars believe it refers to marriage between close relatives. In spite of this uncertainty of translation, John Donahue concludes, "Virtually all New Testament scholars would admit that Matthew represents some kind of exception of an absolute prohibition of divorce."

We find a similar tension in the writings of Paul. In 1 Corinthians, Paul conveys the following teaching: "To those now married, however, I give this command (though it is not mine; it is the Lord's): a wife must not separate from her husband. If she does separate, she must either remain single or become reconciled to him again. Similarly, a husband must not divorce his wife" (7:10–11). While Paul prohibits divorce between two

Christians, he sees marriage between a believer and a non-believer as a separate case. If the unbeliever is willing to live with the believer, no divorce will be allowed. "If the unbeliever wishes to separate, however, let him do so. The believing husband or wife is not bound in such cases. God has called you to live in peace" (7:15). This practice of allowing a divorce if one of the parties converts to Christianity and the other refuses to live peaceably with the convert is called "the Pauline privilege" and is still recognized by the church today.

Those who argue for the indissolubility of the marriage vow advance two types of arguments: scriptural and sacramental. The scriptural evidence has been presented. Supporters of the church's position contend that the original teaching of Jesus, found in both Paul's first letter to the Corinthians and Mark's gospel, absolutely prohibits the divorce of baptized Christians. They also insist that the Christian understanding of commitment is rooted in the central biblical theme of covenant. It is for this reason that the author of the letter to the Ephesians relates the marriage covenant between husband and wife to the covenant between Christ and the church (cf. 5:25–32). The second argument is that Catholic sacramental theology precludes the possibility of divorce. Catholics understand sacraments to be occasions of transformation. For example, Catholics believe that at the eucharist the bread and wine become the body and blood of Christ. Baptism is another example of this transformation. A person's essence is changed through baptism. For this reason in the Roman Catholic Church baptism is received only once. In the same way, the sacrament of marriage transforms the identity of bride and groom. They are united, made one, in marriage. "From a valid marriage there arises between the spouses a bond which of its own nature is permanent and exclusive. Moreover, in Christian marriage the spouses are by a special sacrament strengthened and, as it were, consecrated for the duties and dignity of their state" (Canon 1134).

Those who wish to allow divorce and remarriage in the Roman Catholic Church advance two arguments of their own: the first is pastoral, the second is philosophical.

The pastoral argument contends that the absolute prohibition against divorce and remarriage alienates many loyal Catholics from the church they love. Divorced Catholics who wish to remarry face the troublesome consequence of being barred from the sacramental life of the church. Many feel that their divorce is regarded by the church hierarchy as an unforgivable sin. Often their frustration turns to resentment and they leave the church. Those who favor the allowance of divorce and remarriage call for greater pastoral sensitivity on the part of the church leadership. They argue that a more lenient attitude toward divorce and remarriage would keep many divorced Catholics in the church.

The philosophical argument concerns the nature of promises. While some philosophers argue that promises may never be broken, others argue that no promise, even a sacred one, is absolute. If a radical shift in circumstances occurs after a promise is made, it is reasonable, some would argue, to presume that the promise is no longer binding. Suppose, for example, that a person promises to attend a testimonial dinner for a very dear friend. The person who made the promise then suddenly falls ill and is hospitalized a day before the dinner. This person's absence from the dinner would not be considered a case of a broken promise. Those advancing this argument conclude that it is possible that under certain conditions release from a promise, even a sacred one, is morally justifiable.

The possibility of release from a promise or vow constitutes one of the major pastoral concerns of the Roman Catholic Church today. If the conditions in which a vow was professed radically change, may a person be released from the vow? Many of the sisters and brothers who left religious life in the years following Vatican II felt that the order in which they had taken their vows had changed beyond recognition. Many couples who file for divorce do so on the grounds of "irreconcilable differences." They have "grown apart" and the relationship they once enjoyed has completely deteriorated. We will examine two opposing views toward the nature of such vowed commitments and the possibility of release from these promises.

The first view holds that vowed commitments are absolute. Those in this school of thought fear the trivialization of solemn promises. If a person has freely undertaken a vow to life-long fidelity, then the person must fulfill the obligation. In a marriage, for example, both husband and wife vow to love and honor one another in good times and in bad, in sickness and in health, all the days of their lives. If a wife should suffer from a terminal illness, her husband is required to do everything within his power to care for her. Another concern expressed by advocates of this view is that those who take such vows fail to realize the full range of obligations these vows entail. When entering religious life, for example, sisters and brothers commit themselves to the support and care of other members of their community. A couple who has brought children into the world has an obligation to assist each other in the care of the children and they have an obligation to the children to love, guide, and encourage them. Once they have made a solemn promise, people are obligated to fulfill all the duties which follow from that commitment.

The second view holds that there is no moral obligation to continue in relationships which are destructive. If a religious community loses sight of its mission or if the atmosphere is no longer conducive to the development of one's spirituality, then a sister or brother may leave the order. If in the course of a marriage the relationship between the husband and wife breaks down and marriage counseling proves unsuccessful, then the couple is no longer *obligated* to stay together. If they choose to remain married for reasons of their own, that is, of course, their right, but they are not obligated to do so. Those who argue this position likewise add that this recognition does not undercut the moral weight of vows or promises. This position does not lead to the trivialization of vows or promises; rather, it safeguards their moral significance by carefully limiting the circumstances in which they may morally be broken.

The issue of release from vows centers on the place of the self in moral consideration. What obligations do we have to ourselves? On the one hand, there are many who insist that all commitments are made against the backdrop of human wholeness. The purpose of commitment is to help, not harm individuals; to move persons forward, not hinder them. A commitment certainly places demands on a person, but if, on a very fundamental level, that person's dignity is not respected, then he or she should end the relationship. On the other hand, there are many who insist that commitment requires self-sacrifice. Those on this side of the debate caution that the appeal to the needs of the self can often disguise simple selfishness. Christians are called to serve God and neighbor above self. Furthermore, while self-fulfillment is certainly crucial, our commitments to others in our lives restrict the ways in which such fulfillment may be realized. For example, a husband or wife cannot morally justify extramarital affairs on the basis of human fulfillment. Self-fulfillment, while extremely important, is not always the decisive factor in moral deliberation.

This question of release from commitment raises questions about the purpose of law, and, more specifically, church law. There are two points of view concerning church law. The first holds that the laws of the church are ideals toward which we should strive. The second holds that the laws of the church are basic requirements for church membership. These two points of view offer differing opinions about how such release should be viewed by the church. In the first perspective, there is a sense that as ideals, the laws are not absolutely binding. The church stands in the paradoxical position of upholding the laws as ideals while recognizing that human imperfection may prevent many from living the ideal. Advocates of this position cite Jesus' admonitions in the sermon on the mount as examples. Jesus teaches, "You have heard the commandment, 'An eye for an eye, a tooth for a tooth.' But what I say to you is: offer no resistance to injury. When a person strikes you on the right cheek, turn and offer him the other" (Mt 5:38–39). The church recognizes that this admonition is not absolute. If it were, all Roman Catholics would be pacifists. Instead, the church has a just war tradition which identifies certain conditions in which Catholics may participate in warfare. The second position sees church laws as binding on all those who choose to belong to the church. As in a legal contract, for example, specific obligations are undertaken by each party. The failure to uphold one's side of a bargain is a serious breach of a contract. In the same way, failure to abide by church law is a serious transgression.

Both perspectives toward church law have their relative strengths and weaknesses. The strength of the first perspective is that it allows for human shortcomings, but as we have noted earlier, it can justify one's own self-interest. The second perspective preserves the integrity of the law, but seems to overlook the struggles endured by humans.

In dealing with cases of those seeking release from vowed commitment, the church is torn between the demands of justice and mercy. Justice requires that all persons be treated equally. The virtue of justice is that it is blind. The blindness of justice ensures that those who possess social standing or economic clout will not be granted any advantage over those who do not enjoy those benefits. The virtue of mercy is that it is compassionate. The compassion called for in the name of mercy ensures that the assessment of human actions not become depersonalized. These two necessary poles create a tension in which human judgments are to be made.

The scriptural story of the woman caught in the act of adultery (Jn 8:1–11) illustrates well the tension between justice and mercy. In this story the authorities bring the woman before Jesus and ask, in hope of trapping him, what punishment the woman deserves. The punishment prescribed in the law was clear: "If a man commits adultery with his neighbor's wife, both the adulterer and the adulteress shall be put to death" (Lv 20:10) and "If a man is discovered having relations with a woman who is married to another, both the man and the woman with whom he had relations shall die. Thus shall you purge the evil from your midst" (Dt 22:22). After pausing to scribble in the sand, Jesus responds cleverly to those who brought the woman before him: "Let the man among you who has no sin be the first to cast a stone at her" (Jn 8:7). Afterward Jesus resumes his scribbling. The final verses of the story capture the tension between justice and mercy. The audience around Jesus quietly disperses, leaving the woman standing before Jesus himself. "Jesus finally straightened up and said to her, 'Woman, where did they all disappear to? Has no one condemned you?' 'No one sir,' she answered. Jesus said, 'Nor do I condemn you. You may go. But from now on, avoid this sin' " (Jn 8:10–11).

Those who value mercy emphasize Jesus' refusal of condemnation while those who value justice highlight his command to her to desist in her adulterous activity. Jesus seems to combine here a sense of compassion with a respect for the law. Unfortunately, then as now, this balance is difficult to obtain. If the church ignores its own laws or applies them inconsistently, it is guilty of hypocrisy. If the church does not consider the circumstances of people's lives, it is guilty of insensitivity. The church risks, on the one hand, alienating many from their spiritual home and, on the other hand, failing to stand by its sacramental understanding of commitment. Like Jesus, the church must balance justice and mercy if it is to deal successfully with the dilemma of Christian commitment.

DISCUSSION QUESTIONS

1. Should divorced Roman Catholics be allowed to be remarried in the church?
2. Should laicized priests who are married be allowed to resume their priestly duties?
3. Is an annulment just a "Catholic divorce"?
4. What obligations do we have to ourselves in a vowed commitment?
5. Are the laws of the church ideals or requirements?

SUGGESTED READING

The official Roman Catholic understanding of marriage is found in paragraphs 47–52 of the *Pastoral Constitution on the Church in the Modern World (Gaudium et spes)* found in standard collections of Vatican II documents.

Divorce and Remarriage in the Catholic Church (Mahwah: Paulist Press, 1988) by Gerald D. Coleman, S.S. is a helpful text and contains a useful bibliography.

Discussions of divorce and remarriage can also be found in Kevin T. Kelly's *Divorce and Second Marriage: Facing the Challenge* (New York: Seabury, 1982), and Stephen J. Kelleher's *Divorce and Remarriage for Catholics?* (Garden City: Doubleday, 1973).

For a general discussion of commitment see *Caring and Commitment: Learning to Live the Love We Promise* by Lewis Smedes (San Francisco: Harper & Row, 1988).

Advanced theological students should see the widely discussed *Habits of the Heart: Individualism and Commitment in American Life* by Robert Bellah, et al. (Berkeley: University of California Press, 1985).

See also *Love and Conflict: A Covenantal Model of Christian Ethics* (Nashville: Abingdon Press, 1984) by Joseph L. Allen and *Personal Commitments: Beginning, Keeping, Changing* (San Francisco: Harper & Row, 1986) by Margaret Farley.

The Dilemma of Faith and Reason

Should we "just believe" and not think?

"The apostles said to the Lord, 'Increase our faith,' and he answered: 'If you had the faith the size of the mustard seed, you could say to this sycamore, "Be uprooted and transplanted into the sea," and it would obey you' " (Lk 17:5–6). This dramatic saying of Jesus is but one of his many teachings underscoring the importance of faith. The story of Peter walking with Jesus on the water cleverly illustrates this theme: as Peter falters in his faith, he begins to sink (cf. Mt 14:28–32). In the accounts of Jesus' healings, the gospel writers frequently make a connection between the faith of the person and Jesus' success with the miracle (cf. Mk 6:1–6; Mt 9:22). Along with the admonitions to trust in the Lord, the scriptures also contain numerous passages which extol the pursuit of wisdom as a noble endeavor. For centuries, women and men of great religious faith have pursued greater insight into the mystery of God through the use of reason. These people look upon reason as a gift from the creator which leads them back to the creator. In this chapter we inquire into the relationship between faith and reason. Are faith and reason complements or opposites?

In the first century the catalyst for the debate between faith and reason was the encounter with a religious and philosophical movement known as gnosticism. The various sects associated with gnosticism promised privileged knowledge (*gnosis* = knowledge) through participation in ritual activity or by secret instruction. Gnostic tendencies caused great division within the church at Corinth. In gnostic thought, there are levels of understanding of the mysteries of the universe: the greater one's understanding, the closer one is to complete liberation from this world. The various gnostic teachers promised greater knowledge of these mysteries. As a consequence, there was a tendency for followers of a given teacher or participants in a certain cult to look down upon others as less enlightened or less knowledgable. Paul adamantly opposed the importation of these gnostic ideas into the Corinthian church. As a way of countering the gnostic claims, Paul argued that the wisdom of God bears no similarity to the "wisdom" which the Corinthians value so dearly.

Paul's argument to the Corinthians centers on the cross as the means through which God's wisdom was revealed to the world. Paul writes,

> Since in God's wisdom the world did not come to know him through "wisdom," it pleased God to save those who believe through the absurdity of the preaching of the gospel. Yes, Jews demand "signs" and Greeks look for "wisdom," but we preach Christ crucified—a stumbling block to the Jews, and an absurdity to Gentiles; but to those who are called, Jews and Gentiles alike, Christ the power of God and the wisdom of God. For God's folly is wiser than men and his weakness more powerful than men (1 Cor 1:21–25).

In contrast to the thinking at Corinth, Paul insists that our "faith rests not on the wisdom of men but on the power of God" (1 Cor 2:5). The power of God in turn appears to many as "absurdity" and "folly." Paul summons the Corinthians to a new understanding of the Christian life based on the absurdity of the cross. In place of factions, a sense of unity, based on the one baptism into Christ, must reign in the Christian community. In place of the egotistic pursuit of "knowledge," the Corinthians must embrace the way of love which places the welfare of neighbor over one's own concerns.

The faith-reason controversy has erupted periodically over the course of Christian history. The circumstances of the disputes vary, but the issues remain in many important ways remarkably similar. Some theologians, echoing Paul, feel that the Christian gospel is an "absurdity." In addition to the crucifixion, the birth of Jesus presents us with an incredible event. The Son of God enters the world in the person of the infant Jesus, wrapped in swaddling clothes in a manger in Bethlehem. The central beliefs of Christianity (e.g. the virgin birth, the resurrection, the Trinity) are profound mysteries which we accept on faith. A second group of theologians maintain that appeals to reason turn our attention away from more reliable sources. For example, if scripture contains all knowledge for salvation, then focusing on the thoughts of philosophers is senseless. If the church teaches all truths necessary for salvation, then the submission of mind and will to the teaching authority of the church is required. Finally, a third group values experience above knowledge. If the experience of union with the Lord is cherished above all else, then Christians should concentrate on the heart and not on the mind. Intellectual pursuits are at best unimportant, and at worse detrimental, to the spiritual life.

While many Christian thinkers have warned against the dangers of an overreliance on reason, others have cautioned against an overreliance on faith. If religious belief becomes solely a matter of faith, then rational arguments have no part to play in the formation or evaluation of religious beliefs. In that case, all objects of belief are equally valid. It would be improper to challenge the rationality of the "religious" beliefs of any group, even if such beliefs promoted white supremacy or child sacrifice. In addition to this negative argument, there are three positive arguments for the use of reason in religious matters.

First of all, if we assume that God's creation is fundamentally good, then the innate desire for knowledge should be seen as a God-given gift. Humanity's curiosity and appetite for knowledge would be seen as a positive force in the world, not only leading to important discoveries in the fields of medicine, mathematics, and physics, but also serving a religious function as well. Since God is the source of all truth, the quest for truth leads back ultimately to the creator. Second, the rational display of religious beliefs makes the Christian faith accessible to non-believers. It provides them with the opportunity to understand the central teachings of Christianity and evaluate the credibility of those beliefs. An approach such as this would attempt to demonstrate the rationality of religious belief, rather than encourage the person to simply accept the teaching on faith alone. Finally, it serves an important function within the Christian community itself. If the church is to address itself to the problems of the day, then the church needs to be a place where thoughtful debate and discussion takes place. This in turn requires painstaking intellectual effort on the part of the participants. The complexities of modern life present the church with a host of problems, and Christians need first to be able to speak meaningfully to one another before they can speak persuasively to the world. As Jesus says, "Can a blind man act as a guide to a blind man? Will they not both fall into a ditch?" (Lk 6:39).

The so-called "proofs" for the existence of God popularized by St. Thomas Aquinas provide an interesting test case for evaluating the extent to which appeals to faith or reason are appropriate. The word "proofs" must be used with some caution. The term "proofs" suggests that no reasonable refutation can be given to the belief. The proofs for the existence of God tend to make more modest claims; they present a case for the reasonableness of the belief that God exists. Of the many proofs offered for God's existence, only two will be discussed here.

These two are often classified as "cosmological proofs." "Cosmological proofs" look to world or universe (*cosmos* = universe) as the basis for the reasonableness of the belief in God's existence. The extent to which these two proofs are persuasive indicates the degree of confidence one places in the ability of reason alone to demonstrate the existence of God.

The two cosmological "proofs" both have a commonsensical tone about them. The first argues from the simple fact that the universe exists. How did the universe come into existence? Scientists believe that the universe resulted from a Big Bang in which gases and elements condensed, heated, and finally exploded, producing the basic material from which our solar system was created. How did the necessary materials come into existence? At this point, it seems two possibilities present themselves. The first is that the universe is eternal—it had no beginning, it simply has existed for all time. The second possibility is that it was created at some point in time. Since both possibilities are reasonable assumptions based on the available data, the Christian claim that the universe was created by a supreme being is a reasonable belief. The second "proof" appeals to the intricate design of the world as the basis for belief in God. The human body, for example, is simply a marvel of nature. The ability to see depends on the coordinated operation of a network of tissues, nerves, chemical and electrical impulses, and blood vessels. How did such design come about? Here again two possibilities present themselves. The first is that such design could be the product of chance or natural evolution. The second option is that such design indicates that the world was created by an intelligent being. The Christian claim that the world was created by an intelligent being, therefore, has credence.

Critics charge that these arguments fail in a number of important ways. First, the most general criticism is that the entire project of attempting to prove God's existence is flawed. It betrays a lack of faith on the part of those who feel such proofs are necessary. As we read in the letter to the Hebrews, "Faith is confident assurance concerning what we hope for, and conviction about things we do not see" (11:1). Faith is by definition the acceptance of the existence of "things we do not see."

The second criticism calls into question the success of such proofs. As mentioned earlier, few theologians would claim that the proofs are watertight. For example, the appeal to the design of the world as the basis for belief in God fails to account for the randomness and chaos which can also be discerned in the world. Natural disasters prevent us from too quickly positing the existence of an all-wise creator. Perhaps it would be more accurate, on the basis of the observation of the world, to posit the existence of a creator who is to some degree imperfect. This does not square with the Christian belief in an all-knowing, all-loving, and all-powerful God.

The third criticism attacks the arguments on religious grounds. The arguments may demonstrate the reasonableness of belief in a first cause in the universe. A first cause may prove interesting to the scientist who wishes to explain the origin of the universe, but the Christian God is not an impersonal being whose sole activity was the creation of the world. The Christian God is concerned about the welfare of humanity and the course of human history. The proofs, even if they are successful, do not approach the God described in the Bible or worshiped in liturgy. This sentiment might well be shared by Blaise Pascal, the brilliant French thinker who recorded on a piece of parchment his own intense experience of God. Pascal sewed this piece of parchment into his coat where it was discovered after his death. One of the lines succinctly states the idea at hand: " 'God of Abraham, God of Isaac, God of Jacob,' not of philosophers and scholars." In this mystical experience, Pascal encountered the personal God proclaimed in scripture, not an abstract philosophical concept.

The faith-reason controversy would not be a controversy if both were seen as complementary. This was the case in the thinking of St. Thomas Aquinas. Aquinas argued that certain truths could be known through reason. Through the revelation of God, we gain a more complete understanding of the truth. Revelation complements, but does not contradict, what we know through reason. For example, through reason alone we can see that there is a first cause; through revelation we know that the first cause is the God proclaimed in scripture.

In the modern age, the faith-reason controversy has spawned a related debate: What is the relationship between religion and science? Galileo's and Darwin's findings directly challenged established Christian beliefs. For example, Darwin's theory of evolution contradicted the biblical accounts of creation. In light of these and other developments, the medieval view of complementary truths proved difficult to preserve. Various positions on the question of the proper relationship between religion and science have arisen since Galileo first turned his telescope to the heavens. One group of thinkers sees no tension at all between religion and science. Three popular responses to the religion-science question fall into this category. The first calls for the complete rejection of the findings of modern science. The fundamentalists, for example, denounce the theory of evolution on the basis that it conflicts with a literal reading of Genesis. Scientific "evidence" has no claim on Christian belief. The second position, equally extreme, calls for a complete acceptance of the findings of modern science. In this case, Christian belief is revised in accordance with the latest scientific findings. A group of thinkers known as the deists compared God to a great watchmaker who created the world, wound it up, and let it run according to certain laws. The God of deism does not interfere with the laws of nature, nor does that God demonstrate any genuine concern for humanity. The deists, and others of similar thinking, held science to be the supreme criterion of truth, and all beliefs were subjected to the findings of modern science. The third position sees science and religion as separate and distinct fields. They neither confirm nor deny the beliefs of the other. As Galileo once remarked, "The Bible tells us how to go to heaven, not how the heavens go." All three positions do not allow for genuine exchange between science and religion. The first position holds that science is erroneous, the second that science is superior, and the third that science is separate.

A second group of thinkers feels that scientists and believers should enter into dialogue with one another. This group accepts both science and religion as sources of truth and relates the two without immediately allowing the claims of one to overrule the claims of the other. The first example of this type of dialogue between science and religion might be labeled the "corroboration" model. In this approach, religious thinkers identify features of scientific thought which they feel corroborate Christian claims about reality. For example, some thinkers relate the claims of those who have undergone near-death experiences to Christian claims about the afterlife. Another example of this type of dialogue could be called the "mutually dependent" model of dialogue. Here science and religion participate as equal partners in conversation dealing with the gathering and use of scientific data. Is it proper to perform some types of human experimentation in order to advance medical knowledge? If so, under what conditions can such experimentation take place? Are there ethical limitations to genetic engineering?

How can technological advances best improve the quality of life for the world's inhabitants? Researchers dealing with military and pharmaceutical products confront particularly perplexing ethical questions. The absence of dialogue between science and religion could result in the misuse or exploitation of scientific advance.

The faith-reason controversy boils down to two competing views of the Christian life. Each offers a different response to the mysteries of the Christian faith. Those who stress the importance of faith look upon those mysteries with respect and awe. They accept them as one would accept a precious gift. They give thanks for the gift which they have undeservedly received. Those who emphasize reason look upon the mysteries of the faith with fascination. The allure of those mysteries compels these Christians to probe them more deeply. The question arises from a desire to understand more fully the mysteries of the faith. The Christian life for them is a constant exploration of the richness of God's revelation. Both parties present attractive versions of the Christian life. The preference for one over the other determines, in part, how one resolves the dilemma between faith and reason.

DISCUSSION QUESTIONS

1. Does a reliance on faith diminish the significance of reason and vice versa?
2. Can we prove God's existence?
3. Is it possible to accept the findings of modern science and believe in the God proclaimed in scripture?

4. In religious matters, is it better to accept or to question?
5. Respond to Paul's claim, "We walk by faith, not by sight" (2 Cor 5:7).
6. If faith stands at one end of a continuum, what stands at the other end? Doubt? Certainty?

SUGGESTED READING

Two encyclopedia articles provide fine summaries of the issues, though the terminology is at times technical: "Faith and Reason" in the *Catholic Encyclopedia* and "Faith and Reason" in the *New Dictionary of Theology* (Leicester, England: InterVarsity Press, 1988).

The most important recent work on faith development has been done by James Fowler. For a readable introduction to his thought, see *Life Maps: Conversations on the Journey of Faith* by Jim Fowler and Sam Keen (Waco: Word Books, 1978).

For a review of the different possible relations between science and religion, see *Science and Religion* in the Opposing Viewpoints Series, edited by David L. Bender and Bruno Leone (St. Paul: Greenhaven Press, 1981).

The Dilemma of Continuity and Change

Should Christianity change with the times?

The final theological dilemma focuses our attention on the future course of Christian theology. This discussion serves as a fitting ending since it recalls many of the earlier dilemmas. As we move through history new ideas emerge and old ways of thinking become obsolete; consequently, new ways of expressing traditional ideas are needed. The final dilemma is rooted in the tension between fidelity to the past and openness to the future or, in brief, between continuity and change.

The presence of both the priest and prophet in the Hebrew scriptures serves as a reminder of the need for both continuity and change. The priest was linked with the temple or sanctuary where he performed the ritual activities prescribed by the law. The office of priesthood was hereditary. One did not become a priest—one was born a priest. The priest was the only suitable person to serve as the mediator between God and the people. The priesthood embodied order, tradition, and stability. The prophets, on the other hand, could come from any social background. Nor were they confined to one hereditary line. The prophet need not be associated with the temple or any sanctuary. The prophet criticized the political leaders for their failure to rely upon Yahweh and chided the religious leaders for overlooking the needs of the poor. Whereas the priest treasured continuity, the prophet called for change. "Remember not the events of the past, the things of long ago consider not. See, I am doing something new!" (Is 43:18–19a). While this distinction between priest and prophet is not hard and fast (e.g. Ezekiel was both priest and prophet), the two impulses are clearly evident in the biblical writings. The biblical authors coupled a deep respect for tradition with a high regard for protest.

The tension between continuity and change lies at the very heart of the theological enterprise. We began our examination of the theological dilemmas by defining theology as "critical reflection upon religious beliefs and practices." The activity of "critical reflection" has to do with evaluating religious beliefs and practices. Theologian A offers his evaluation; theologian B offers her evaluation. Who is right? By what standards do we say one theological position is better than another? Two major elements factor into the evaluation of theological statements. The first is fidelity to the central tenets of Christianity. To advocate that Jesus was a wise teacher but nothing more than that is simply outside the realm of possibility for the orthodox Christian theologian. To deny that Jesus was the messiah would be to deny the keystone of our faith as Christians. The first condition of a sound theological position is, therefore, faithfulness to the central teachings of the Christian tradition. The second condition is no less important than the first. The Christian faith must be presented in terms which contemporary Christians understand. If people do not grasp the meaning of the traditional statements, then theologians must either explicate the meaning of the traditional language or devise new formulations. This second condition is, therefore, intelligibility. Sound theological statements must be both faithful to the basic tenets of the faith and intelligible and meaningful to contemporary Christians.

It is this dual task of re-presentation and reformulation which creates a tension for theologians. We have explored this tension in the earlier discussions. In brief, conservatives fear the loss of orthodoxy. Christianity is not created anew with each generation; rather, the truths of the faith are passed on from one generation to the next. In order to protect these truths, the conservative favors continuity with the tradition. Liberals, by contrast, fear that Christianity will become irrelevant to the lives of Christians. If the traditional language no longer proves meaningful, then new ways of expression must be found. In order to make Christianity relevant, the liberal favors change. The theologian must attend to the legitimate concerns of both parties. Theologians can not simply throw out the old in favor of the new nor can they simply ignore the audience to whom they are writing. Theology requires skillful maneuvering between the demands of faithfulness to the tradition and adaptation to the present moment.

The contemporary discussion of the eucharist illustrates well the tension between faithfulness and adaptation. The traditional Roman Catholic teaching concerning the eucharist is that Christ is present in the consecrated bread and wine. The teaching itself, known as transubstantiation, employs categories of thought borrowed from Aristotle. The basic distinction underlying the doctrine of transubstantiation is between substance and accidents. The substance of an object is absolutely essential to the object. If the substance of an object is changed, then the object becomes something different. Accidents are non-essential qualities. For example, a dog may have brown hair or black hair. Color is an accident. One can alter the color of the hair of a dog and the animal is still a dog. The substance of the dog remains unchanged even if the color of its hair is changed. The doctrine of transubstantiation teaches that the bread and wine are transformed through the consecration at mass. The elements of bread and wine still possess the characteristics associated with bread and wine (color, taste, etc.), but their substance has been changed. The accidents remain the same, but the substance has changed. Though the elements retain the appearance of bread and wine, the substance becomes the body and blood of Christ.

If the doctrine of transubstantiation is intelligible and meaningful to contemporary Catholics, then no major reformulation of the doctrine is required. Suppose, however, that the language of transubstantiation is alien to contemporary Catholics. The theologian has a number of options, but here we will concentrate on two of them. First, the theologian may employ different language to "say the same thing" about the eucharist. Instead of the language of transubstantiation, the theologian may speak of Christ's real presence in terms of symbolic re-enactment, that is, by gathering together as a community of believers and recalling the words of Jesus at the last supper, we experience his presence in a unique and powerful way. The theological question is: Does this reformulation adequately restate the doctrine of transubstantiation? Have we lost something in the translation? The second option is to highlight dimensions of the teaching about the eucharist which seem more meaningful to our day and age. For example, given the problem of world hunger, theologians may emphasize the need for Christians to share their bread with those in need in all parts of the world. This approach highlights ideas which complement rather than contradict the traditional teaching. Both approaches attempt to preserve continuity with the tradition.

The more difficult problems arise when the proposed solution calls for discontinuity with the tradition. Two particularly provocative instances of this type of solution concern the ordination of women to the priesthood and the use of feminine language to speak about God.

The arguments against the ordination of women can be grouped into three types: scriptural, theological, and traditional. The scriptural argument insists that although Jesus certainly challenged many of the customs of the day, he nonetheless did not call a woman to be one of the twelve. The theological argument states that since the priest represents Christ, only males can be priests. The final argument appeals to the weight of tradition. The Roman Catholic Church has at no time in its history ordained women. Those favoring women's ordination find these arguments deficient. They argue on scriptural grounds that the exclusion of women from the priesthood violates the scriptural premise that all are one in Christ. "There does not exist among you Jew or Greek, slave or freemen, male or female. All are one in Christ Jesus" (Gal 3:28). Nor is there a direct scriptural prohibition against women's ordination. Theologically, critics charge that all those who are baptized should be entitled to full participation in the life of the church. Finally, they argue that the tradition stands in need of correction. Just as other practices have been changed or dropped over time, so too should the ban on women's ordination be lifted.

Theological debates are often far removed from what goes on during mass on Sunday morning. The resolution of the question of women's ordination, however, directly impacts the life of the ordinary Catholic in the parish. It would allow or continue to disallow women to preside at the eucharist. The stakes are high in the debate between continuity and change. If we err, we either have destroyed a noble tradition of the church or have unjustly barred a person from responding to her priestly calling. This debate presents the church with a quandary, one which is not only "theoretical" but of immense practical significance for the life of the church.

The use of feminine language about God creates even greater debate than the question of the ordination of women. Is it permissible in liturgy to substitute the word Mother in those places where we have traditionally used the word Father? Is it acceptable to use feminine imagery about God in the homily? We will explore two of the arguments proposed by those favoring the use of feminine language about God. The first argument is as follows. God has no gender. God is neither male nor female. All talk about God is by way of analogy. God is obviously not a father in a literal sense. God is a father in that God possesses qualities which we traditionally associate with fathers, e.g. power, protection. God also possesses qualities which we

traditionally associate with mothers, e.g. God is caring and nur-
turing. The use of feminine language about God calls to our
attention those qualities of God which are downplayed or ig-
nored when God is addressed exclusively in masculine
language.

The second argument involves three steps. The first step
deals with the message of Jesus. Jesus proclaimed a vision of
the kingdom of God in which all injustice and oppression would
be overturned. As Christians we commit ourselves to overturning injustice and oppression as we await the arrival of this new
age promised by Jesus. This understanding of Jesus' message
sets the stage for the second claim. There exists a direct relationship between (a) language and (b) social structure and self-
image. In many work places the use of the words "officers" and
"subordinates" has given way to "teams." Borrowed from the
military, the terms "officers" and "subordinates" denote regi-
mentation, discipline, and order. Though these are honorable
qualities, the terminology establishes a rigid distinction of roles.
The "subordinates" follow the orders of the "officer." Given
this power arrangement, subordinates would feel uncomfort-
able offering suggestions to the officer. This structure diminishes the amount of creative input and tends to lower employee
morale. The word "team" suggests a more collaborative approach to decision making. The team would have a leader, but
the distance between that person and the other members is
lessened. The point is obvious: when language changes, the
relations between people often also change. The final step in
the argument is perhaps the most controversial. Those advocating the use of feminine language for God argue that the exclusive use of masculine language about God has created a patriarchical social arrangement. Since an egalitarian social structure
is more in keeping with the message of Jesus, we need to em-

ploy language which fosters this egalitarian understanding of the male-female relationship.

Opponents charge that the masculine language about God comes from scripture and has been incorporated into the liturgy of the church. Expressions such as "Our Father, who art in heaven" cannot be altered. The "Our Father" enjoys this privileged status for the simple fact that Jesus taught these words to us. These words naturally have been integrated into the life of the church. We do not have the right to alter that which we do not like. For example, John's gospel contains a number of negative references to "the Jews." After the crucifixion, "the disciples had locked the doors of the place where they were for fear of the Jews" (Jn 20:19). As Christians have begun to deal with the question of anti-semitism more directly, these passages have become more troubling. The tendency would be to remove those passages or substitute "the crowds" for "the Jews." By keeping such passages intact, the discussion of the issues of anti-semitism or racism or sexism continues.

The greater concern of the conservatives involves the question of identity. Change is inevitable, but some change is good and other change is not. In the biological realm, we observe the development of organic life. We recognize the budding and blossoming of flowers and the growth of animals into maturity as part of the natural process of development. Disease also changes life forms, but in a destructive way. The question here is: Are there any changes which, if implemented, would either prove detrimental to Christianity or alter it to the point that it is unrecognizable? For example, it seems unimaginable that Quakers could abandon their pacifism and remain in any sense of the term "Quakers." Their pacifism follows from their most cherished commitments to justice and peace. The surrender of those commitments would constitute a fundamental break with the Quaker tradition. Applying this to the discussion at hand, would the ordination of women "be a step in the wrong direction"? Would the ordination of women create an entirely new form of Roman Catholicism? Would something significant or essential be lost?

This leads us to another difficult question: Who decides when change is positive and when it is negative? This question is particularly vexing because change is not always best evaluated in terms of the short term consequences. Changes which meet with initial resistance often in the long run prove extremely beneficial to the life of the church. Who decides? Here again liberals and conservatives offer different responses. The conservatives, emphasizing the need for continuity, usually accept the leaders of the church as the definitive authorities in this matter. As guardians of the tradition, the pope and the bishops are entrusted with safeguarding the faith of the church. The conservatives regard the decisions of the pope and bishops as binding upon all the faithful. For example, when the mass was changed from Latin to the vernacular, the conservatives accepted the change, though many disagreed with the change. The liberals, emphasizing the need for relevance, look to the laypeople for their reaction to a new practice or idea. If the faithful accept the practice or idea, then the liberals look upon that as a confirmation of the acceptability of the innovation. The birth control question which we discussed earlier provides the best example of a teaching which a good number of lay Catholics choose not to follow. Liberals would argue that "the church" has rejected the teaching on birth control since "the church" is to be understood as the entire people of God.

Both liberals and conservatives have legitimate concerns about the future of Christianity. The liberals are correct when they say that new forms of expression provide the Christian community with opportunities for gaining new insights into old ideas. By adding a new perspective on an ancient belief or practice, theologians help us explore more deeply the mysteries of our faith. The conservatives are correct when they point out the benefit of a common theological language and the religious appeal of our participation in a tradition which stretches back over the centuries. This problem of deciding which changes are good and which are not will persist as long as the church continues to live and struggle on its pilgrim way.

Discussion Questions

1. What is more important: fidelity to the tradition or relevance to the present time? Why?
2. Are there any expressions used frequently in church which you do not understand?
3. Are there any teachings of the church which you feel are outdated?
4. Should women be ordained to the priesthood? Why? Why not?
5. Should we use feminine language about God?
6. Is the future of the church bright or bleak?

Suggested Readings

Faith Rediscovered: Coming Home to Catholicism (Mahwah: Paulist Press, 1987) by Lawrence S. Cunningham and *What Are the Theologians Saying?* (Dayton: Pflaum Press, 1970) by Monika Hellwig both deal in a popular style with the question of changes in the church.

Richard P. McBrien's two-volume work *Catholicism* (Minneapolis: Winston Press, 1980) and Thomas Bokenkotter's
Essential Catholicism: Dynamics and Faith and Belief
(Garden City: Doubleday, 1985), two fine recent discussions of Catholicism, both acknowledge the tension between continuity and change. See Chapter One of McBrien
and the preface of Bokenkotter.

Advanced theological students would benefit from reading
Langdon Gilkey's *Catholicism Confronts Modernity: A
Protestant View* (New York: Seabury, 1975) and Peter L.
Berger's *The Heretical Imperative: Contemporary Possi-
bilities of Religious Affirmation* (Garden City: Anchor
Press, 1979).